BATMAN FOREVER™

BATMAN FOREVER™

THE OFFICIAL MOVIE BOOK

MICHAEL SINGER

MANDARIN

Commissioning Editor **Julian Coningsby-Brown**

Design **Sue Michniewicz**

Production **Melanie Frantz**

First published in Great Britain 1995

by Mandarin Paperbacks

an imprint of Reed Consumer Books Limited

Michelin House, 81 Fulham Road, London SW3 6RB

and Auckland, Melbourne, Singapore and Toronto

ISBN 0 7493 2280 2

Printed in the United States

ACKNOWLEDGEMENTS

How do you thank an entire motion picture company? By just doing it, I suppose. And so, my thanks to the entire *Batman Forever* cast and crew – from director Joel Schumacher and producer Peter Macgregor-Scott to the guards at the soundstage doors – for their unstinting cooperation, particularly the 40 tolerant persons who took time out from demanding, mid-production duties for time-consuming interviews.

I'm tremendously grateful to what I'll call the *Batman Forever* Support Group for keeping me propped up on days when my eyes resembled bloodshot saucers. This heroic team of friends and co-workers included – but were not exclusive to – Sarah Knight, Lisa Reardon, Bettina Rose, Nick Berreau, Reg Brack, Mitch Dauterive, Christine Fransen, Robin Mulcahy, Lisa Ullmann, James Spadafore, Jane Payne, Jim Burns, Linda Fields, Jodi Leesley, Bill Elvin, Alan Edmisten, Petur Hliddal and every single hard-working staff assistant on the film, including Cynthia LaPointe, Benjamin Ballard, Lisa Bloch, Adam Duthie and many more not mentioned by name. Those in individual departments who generously extended themselves include Jill DuDeck and Eli Richbourg of the Art Department and Jo Ann Knox of Visual Effects. But there are so many more unnamed friends and co-workers who also deserve my endless gratitude.

Many thanks to Ralph Nelson for his extraordinary unit photography and unwavering support.

At DC Comics, Dawn Evans and Steve Korté kept the wheels turning and my computer burning. They were great pals and terrific editors. Also at DC, all honor to Phyllis Hume for her delightfully New York-accented advocacy.

At Warner Bros., Charlotte Kandel, John Dartigue, Jill Jacobs and Kim Cannon were elemental in getting this book started *and* finished.

At Reed Illustrated Books in London, Julian Brown and designer Sue Michniewicz brought characteristic British patience to the proceedings.

And at home, my wife Yuko and our daughter Miyako (who chose to enter this world during production of the film and the writing of this book) tolerated my insane hours, incessant key-pounding and oft-times crazed personality. This book is dedicated to them, my two shrine maidens, with consuming love and endless appreciation.

introduction by bob kane

Above: Bob Kane on the set. *Right:* Kane and his wife, the actress Elizabeth Sanders, who portrays "Gossip Gerty" in the film.

When I created Batman at the age of 18, I never, in my wildest imagination, dreamt that the concept would become as popular as it has. I'm not sure that any writer or artist can know in the initial creation of a character how the public will receive it. Did Arthur Conan Doyle know where Sherlock Holmes would go? Did Ian Fleming know how world-famous James Bond would be?

One never knows, does one?

Being a creative artist can be a very introspective, lonely existence. While you're working, you're alone, and you can't have telephones ringing or friends visiting. Sometimes I think that nobody's listening, watching or reading my work ... until I go to a comic book convention and meet the people. Or receive thousands of letters a year from fans all over the world who either want an autograph or drawing. I get some very poignant letters from people whose lives were influenced by the Batman stories and movies. Then I realize that I literally have millions of friends and that Batman has reached all walks of life.

More proof of this wonderful fact is that we now have a brand new film called *Batman Forever*. This movie will look nothing like the previous two. It's an original. And it's not a sequel, but a whole new ballgame, with a new Batman, new villains, new sets and a great new director, Joel Schumacher.

In my personal opinion, I think this movie will be a blowout!

Val Kilmer, the new Batman, is terrific. The first time I saw him on the set, I thought that he embodied every-thing that I perceived when I created Batman 55 years ago. Val has a charming, sophisticated personality as Bruce Wayne, and he looks and acts exactly as Batman should. The rest of the *Batman Forever* cast is sterling. Tommy Lee Jones is an excellent Two-Face, and the phenomenal Jim Carrey is just wonderful as the Riddler. Nicole Kidman is beautiful as the criminal psychiatrist Dr. Chase Meridian, and Chris O'Donnell will be playing Robin without camping it up.

Having had the opportunity to spend time on the *Batman Forever* set, I can tell you that the new Gotham City is utterly fantastic. It's so futuristic and detailed, and quite different from the other two films. The scale of these sets would have been appreciated by Cecil B. DeMille and Michelangelo. And the new Batmobile is also absolutely spectacular.

Seeing what Joel Schumacher and his hand-picked cast are doing on the set makes me very proud to have created this character and the world he inhabits. He will be here long after I'm gone, but I've left my footprint in the sands of time. I wish I could live to be 500 to see more incarnations of the Batman lore, but I guess I can just take in one Batman at a time.

In closing, I'd just like to say thank you to all the fans across the world for the letters I receive. Without these fans, there'd be no Batman to claim. I just hope we'll keep turning out bigger and better Batman movies for you to enjoy ... and I certainly think that's the case with *Batman Forever*.

director Joel Schumacher

a new day for the dark knight

Batman Forever. Scene 164. Bruce Wayne, Gotham's most eligible bachelor multimillionaire industrialist ... Batman by night ... visits the elegant office of the stunningly beautiful Dr. Chase Meridian, an eminent criminal psychiatrist specializing in dual personalities. Bruce has been receiving strange, disturbing riddles at his Wayne Enterprises office, and is seeking clues to the sender's identity. He notices a framed print hanging on the office wall. A bat. "You have a thing for bats?" Bruce asks Dr. Meridian. "That's a Rorschach, Mr. Wayne," Chase responds. "An ink blot. People see what they want." Bruce notices that the framed print is, in fact, just an ink blot.

But he saw a bat within its irregular lines.

It was May 1939 when Bob Kane's nocturnal hero made his smashing debut in Detective Comics #27. Artists, writers, novelists, animators, television and moviemakers have all seen something similar yet distinct in that Rorschach test called Batman. The Dark Knight has been all things to all people, magnificently pliable and subject to change without notice, depending upon individual interpretation, orientation and examination. Batman, in Kane's 1939 version, was "The Bat-Man," inspired by Leonardo da Vinci's notebook sketch of the "Ornithopter" glider, the silent film version of *The Mark of Zorro* and the 1931 film version of Mary Roberts Rinehart's mystery novel, *The Bat Whispers*.

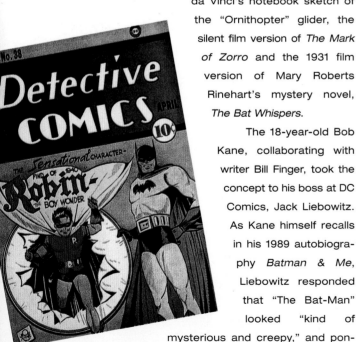

The 18-year-old Bob Kane, collaborating with writer Bill Finger, took the concept to his boss at DC Comics, Jack Liebowitz. As Kane himself recalls in his 1989 autobiography *Batman & Me*, Liebowitz responded that "The Bat-Man" looked "kind of mysterious and creepy," and pondered whether or not the public would like it ... which proved to be one of American cultural history's most rhetorical questions!

Since that fateful day, Batman has morphed into as many variations as its explicator of the moment could conceive, with the Dark Knight personification emerging from the 1980s as the Batman of choice for most of his fans. It was this characterization that captured the imagination of readers in the comic books and graphic novels that followed in the thunderous wake of *Batman: The Dark Knight Returns*, Frank Miller's extraordinary four-part series published in 1986. And it was a variation of this gothic manifestation of Batman that informed Tim Burton's massively successful 1989 Warner Bros. film, *Batman*, and its 1992 follow-up, *Batman Returns*.

Considering the fact that contemporary movie audiences welcomed the two Batman films onto theatre screens to the sweet tune of almost one billion dollars worldwide, a third cinematic opus was inevitable. When Tim Burton decided that two directorial forays into Gotham City had satisfied his own need to explore the legend and lore of Batman, Warner Bros. Chairmen Robert A. Daly and Terry Semel passed the torch to one of Hollywood's most versatile and stylish filmmakers: Joel Schumacher.

schumacher style

Joel Schumacher is that rarity in the movie business ... a director who actually revels in what he does for a living. Gregarious, exuberant, uninhibited, extroverted, razor-sharp and with a lightning-quick wit that is both warm and wicked, Schumacher delights in

the process of filmmaking as only one can who has fulfilled a lifelong dream – that at one time seemed a million light years away. "This is what we do for a living," notes Schumacher matter-of-factly. "If we can't approach it with joy and fun, what's the use of doing it?" Schumacher has now been "doing it" for almost 20 years, with unflagging energy and devotion to his craft.

only four years old, and his mother labored long and hard hours selling dresses to support her family. Young Joel realized at a very early age that he had creative instincts that demanded to be satisfied, and he hoped against hope that motion pictures would eventually be his calling. And they would ... but not before he excelled as one of New York's most prominent designers and boutique owners in the 1960s. Realizing the first stage of his ultimate goal, Schumacher designed costumes for such notable films as *Play It As It Lays*, *The Last of Sheila*, *Blume in Love* and two collaborations with Woody Allen, *Sleeper* and *Interiors*.

Schumacher's dogged determination to direct next led him to discover his considerable talents as a screenwriter on *Sparkle* and *Car Wash*, both of which demonstrated his ability to deftly juggle ensemble stories and characters ... not to mention his uncanny ability to zero in on contemporary pop culture. In fact, Schumacher cheerfully describes himself as a "pop culture sponge." After directing two well-received television movies (*The Virginia Hill Story* and *Amateur Night at the Dixie Bar and Grill*), Schumacher made his feature

Opposite top: Nicole Kidman as Dr. Chase Meridian hones her boxing skills. *Opposite bottom:* First appearance of Robin in Detective Comics #38 (*left*); Joel Schumacher and Jim Carrey (*right*). *This page:* Schumacher with a four-camera set-up (*above*), consulting with Jim Carrey (*right*) and working out a shot with cinematographer Stephen Goldblatt (*below*).

Fatefully, Schumacher and Batman were born in the same year, and the same city – New York – except that Schumacher was born and raised across the East River in the industrial backdrop of Long Island City (which may well have served as his inspiration for the more downtrodden sections of Gotham City). With the IRT elevated subway rumbling overhead, Schumacher escaped into the Sunnyside Theatre – just behind his home – and immersed himself in the movies. "I was one of those kids whose mothers used to have to drag them out of the movie theatre," Schumacher recalls. "I just lived in that theatre!"

And no wonder. Schumacher's father died when Schumacher was

film debut on the comedy-fantasy *The Incredible Shrinking Woman*. But his directing career was truly launched by the raucous ensemble comedy *D.C. Cab* and the decade-defining *St. Elmo's Fire*, writing both films as well.

This was followed by a series of films in all genres, demonstrating Schumacher's versatility with different subject matter, expertise with both camera and actors, and superlative storytelling abilities. *The Lost Boys*, *Cousins*, *Flatliners* and *Dying Young* established Schumacher as a filmmaker to be reckoned with, and his two most recent motion pictures – *Falling Down* and the 1994 summer hit *The Client* – confirmed him critically and lifted him to the very top levels of Hollywood moviemakers.

It was while Schumacher was scouting locations for *The Client* in New Orleans that he was summoned to Warner Bros. in Burbank, California for that life-altering meeting with Bob Daly and Terry Semel, who inquired if he would be interested in directing the new Batman film. "We had a great meeting," says Schumacher, "and I told them that I would love to do the movie ... but only if Tim Burton wanted me to do it. And thankfully, he did."

Some filmmakers might be daunted by the notion that comparisons would be inevitable, particularly since the first two films were so widely seen. But Schumacher was confident that just as Tim Burton brought a particular vision to the character, his own take would be different enough to give audiences a new experience, rather than a re-tread. "I think Tim did a wonderful job with the other movies," notes Schumacher, "but to copy someone isn't really to flatter them. I think it was incumbent upon us to give our own version of the Batman legend, trying to incorporate some of the things Tim started, but also to give it a new, never-before-seen look."

That "look" was developed in collaboration with such highly-respected Hollywood talents as production designer Barbara Ling, cinematographer Stephen Goldblatt, costume designers Bob Ringwood and Ingrid Ferrin, visual effects supervisor John Dykstra and producer Peter Macgregor-Scott supervising an enormous team of experienced artists. The goal was to bring audiences a new concept of the Batman myth, shimmering with color, shadow, light and movement, inspired by the bold artwork of Bob Kane and all his artistic descendants, but wholly original and innovative in and of itself.

It's a new day for the Dark Knight ...

Right: Two-Face from the DC Comics story "Half An Evil" published in 1971.

the riddler ...
two-face ...
and robin!

Batman presented the Joker in the imposing person of Jack Nicholson, and *Batman Returns* gave us Michelle Pfeiffer as Catwoman and Danny DeVito as the Penguin. For *Batman Forever* an early decision was made to continue delighting Batman fans by introducing new interpretations of time-honored characters: arch-villains Two-Face (aka Harvey Dent) and the Riddler, and one young man by the name of Dick Grayson who pierces the lonely crime-fighting world of Batman, and insists on standing by his side in a new guise – Robin.

Curiously, the fascinating, bizarre Two-Face had never been portrayed by a live-action performer in any previously filmed versions before Tommy Lee Jones tore into the role for *Batman Forever*. (Although Billy Dee Williams appeared as the pre-scarred Gotham City District Attorney Harvey Dent in Tim Burton's 1989 *Batman*). Two-Face first appeared in Detective Comics #66 in 1942, but DC Comics gave the character a leave of absence after March 1954, not to recall his dastardly services until 1971. Two-Face is the ultimate divided man, split down the middle in body and soul, one half evil and

the other ... well, *almost* law-abiding. He perceives everything in pairs, the yin/yang of dualities, and allows a flip of his trademark silver coin – with one side as scarred as his face – to make decisions for him. For Two-Face, the coin never lies.

Like the scarred-in-body-and-soul Captain Ahab of Herman Melville's *Moby Dick*, Two-Face is a man obsessed... not with a white whale but with a Dark Knight, whom he blames for the tragic courtroom accident that caused his disfigurement. (Actually Batman was only trying to deflect a bottle of acid that gangster "Boss" Moroni threw at District Attorney Dent.)

The Riddler was born in Detective Comics #140 in 1948, but remarkably enough, underwent a 20-year disappearing act until May 1965. The Prince of Puzzlers' popularity boomed after the character – as portrayed by comedian Frank Gorshin – was the star villain in the January 12, 1966 pilot episode of *Batman*, ABC-TV's spectacularly popular and camped-up rendering of the Caped Crusader. The Riddler proved to be one of the series' favorite arch-villains, and Gorshin repeated his hyperactive characterization in 20th Century-Fox's 1966 feature film designed to cash in on the TV program. With his green, question mark festooned suits and devilishly clever approach to crime, the Riddler has always been one of Gotham's most colorful scoundrels.

And then there's Robin, one of the most legendary figures of comic book history. Since his debut in Detective Comics #38 in April 1940, Robin has inspired spirited debates over everything from the origin of his appellation to whether or not Batman actually needs a partner in the first place.

And so, Joel Schumacher and writer Akiva Goldsman decided to re-invent Robin not only with a strong '90s twist, but an equally solid nod to the hero's origins as outlined more than 50 years before. Robin remains acrobat Dick Grayson, and he enters Batman's life in the same manner as in Detective #38 after his entire family is killed by criminals during a circus performance (in *Batman Forever*, it's Two-Face and his minions who cause the death of Grayson's family). Unlike the Boy

Wonder of the comics – or for that matter, Burt Ward's portrayal of Robin on the Batman television series – Dick Grayson sports a somewhat tougher, more mature edge in the new film, as might realistically befit a young man who's spent his entire life as a traveling circus gypsy. When Dick finally teams with Batman, it makes for a true Dynamic Duo for this era ... and perhaps for the next one as well.

Besides Burt Ward, Robin has also been portrayed by Douglas Croft in the 1943 Batman movie serial that starred Lewis Wilson as Batman, and by John Duncan in the 1949 *Batman and Robin* serial that toplined Robert Lowery as the Caped Crusader.

Actually, all of the above – Batman, Robin, Two-Face and the Riddler – have also been seen in Warner Bros. Animation's Emmy Award-winning TV show *The Adventures of Batman and Robin*, which premiered in September 1992. The Dark Knight was also imaginatively displayed in Warner's 1993 animated feature *Batman: Mask of the Phantasm*.

Batman and his various friends and foes have lasted through the Second World War, the Korean War, the Vietnam War, the advent of space travel, eleven U.S. presidents, Elvis Presley, the Beatles, the fall of Communism in the Soviet Union and Eastern Europe and more earthshaking events than can be recounted in a volume the size of the *Encyclopaedia Britannica*.

But in a universe of uncertainties, you can reliably bet on this ... Gotham's Dark Knight goes ever onward, adaptable to all media, in all seasons ... and for all generations.

Top: Two-Face on the cover of Detective Comics, November 1987. *Above center:* The first appearance of the Riddler in Detective Comics #140. *Below center:* Batman and Robin together in 1968. *Bottom:* An August 1966 Detective Comics Batman cover.

It's a sizzling Monday morning in Los Angeles, August 1994. In an air conditioned conference room tucked away on the side of Warner Bros.' Stage 15, minds are ablaze. It's a pre-production department head session, a time for discussing the nuts and bolts of physical production that will make "real" what previously has up until now been pure illusion.

PRE-PRODUCTION
the
team
assembles

At the head of a long table sit director Joel Schumacher and producer Peter Macgregor-Scott. They are surrounded by team leaders including first assistant director Bill Elvin, cinematographer Stephen Goldblatt, production designer Barbara Ling, costume designers Bob Ringwood and Ingrid Ferrin, screenwriter Akiva Goldsman, visual effects supervisor John Dykstra, special effects supervisor Tommy Fisher, production manager Ralph Burris, propmaster Brad Einhorn, stunt coordinator Conrad Palmisano, script supervisor Sharron Reynolds-Enriquez and location managers Laura Sode-Matteson and Val Kim, among others. Production illustrations are displayed around the room to give a sense of what's to come. It's a free and open atmosphere for departments to coordinate their efforts, essential for a production of this size.

Schumacher, as always, is informal and often outrageously funny; he's also entirely in command and meticulously organized. "The *people* will move the story," he declares, "not pyrotechnics. All stunts and action that don't serve character are *out*! The spotlight will be on the principals. Always do what's exciting, but be practical."

In discussing the action scenes with stunt coordinator Palmisano, the director says, "The audience knows that Batman isn't going to be killed, so the only fun they can have is if they see something that's different and exciting. We have to think up new ways for Batman to make his entrances, new ways for him to fight."

To another query regarding a scene's realistic credibility, Schumacher drolly replies, "You know what? Christopher Reeve *cannot* really fly. We're making *movies*!"

What does Joel Schumacher want from his creative staff? As he cogently puts it, "More cluck for our buck!" In other words, take it to the limit, and then push it over the edge ... but within professional reason. And *never* forget the audience!

re-inventing batman

Joel Schumacher never does forget the audience, because he's never separated himself from "them." In fact, Schumacher often notes that he *is* "them." "The only thing I love doing more than going to the movies," he says, "is *making* movies!"

Schumacher certainly loved the idea of making a Batman movie. Recalls the director, "I was always a Batman fan. I've always thought that the series was sexier, darker, iconoclastic, and more rock 'n' roll in a sense. I've always loved the fact that Batman is just a human being, without superpowers, with a troubled past. He's a flawed person who struggles with dark foes, inwardly as well as in the night streets of Gotham City."

Schumacher's strong art background deepened his appreciation for the striking visual traditions established by the Batman comics and graphic novels, and he felt encouraged to invent a completely new version of the Dark Knight on screen. "Hopefully, the audience will have a visual ride as well as an engaging story. Because I think you owe it to people when you're doing a live-action version of a comic book character.

"And I think the word *comic* is important to this project," adds Schumacher. "All the characters have their own sense of humor, and of course, we have Jim Carrey and

Left: Batman dispatches two of Two-Face's thugs at the Gotham Bank raid. *Opposite top:* Joel Schumacher briefs Drew Barrymore. *Opposite bottom:* Tommy Lee Jones as Two-Face.

Tommy Lee Jones as the Riddler and Two-Face to add their own dark comedy to the film.

"After all," reminds the director, "they *are* called *comic* books!"

Just as *Batman* and *Batman Returns* resulted from the singular vision of Tim Burton, so would *Batman Forever* emerge from the remarkably fertile imagination of Joel Schumacher. Thus, after the director accepted Warner Bros. Chairmen Bob Daly and Terry Semel's invitation to direct the film, one of Schumacher's first orders of business was to bring into the process a young writer named Akiva Goldsman, who was then working with him in Memphis on the screenplay for *The Client*. A script for the new Batman film, written by Lee Batchler and Janet Scott Batchler, had already been submitted to the studio,

Schumacher felt that his young collaborator could further infuse the story with his own passion and talent.

And nobody could have been more pleasantly surprised by the offer than Goldsman himself, a lifelong comic book collector and Batman fan.

brooklyn to gotham

"It never entered my mind that I would work on *Batman Forever*," notes the Brooklyn-born Goldsman, "because I was still on *The Client* and work on the Batman script had to commence immediately. But I thought it was a spectacular project for Joel to do, because he has a set of remarkable talents that force you to engage the screen emotionally, visually and intellectually. Tim Burton, I think did an extraordinary job, but he was now ready to pass on the torch ... and I thought no one could be a better bearer of that torch than Joel. We talked and fantasized about the movie, and then both went on with our lives. Later on, I got a phone call from Joel, and he invited me to join him in continuing to develop *Batman Forever*. I simply sat with my mouth open!"

Schumacher recognized that with Goldsman's lifelong interest in comic books – and his unique background working in the mental health field – he had found the perfect person to help him create a new Batman for the '90s. "At heart," comments the director, "*Batman Forever* is a story about duality. Every one of these characters has a split personality. It's almost like making a movie with ten protagonists rather than five!"

Goldsman's insights into the characters that populate the film reveal his thoughtful approach to the material. "Batman is, of course, one of the darkest super heroes available to us," observes the screenwriter. "He has always seemed to me a man driven by guilt. Bruce Wayne has a tremendous trauma in his past which seems to be unresolved. This has resulted in a schism in his personality, a kind of refined, well-behaved do-gooder by day, and a kind of obsessive avenger by night.

"What could be more compelling than that? How do we better understand the character of Bruce Wayne and Batman? For me, it was to again return to that trauma and explore it more fully. And to try and empathize with Bruce Wayne and see how the trauma might, in a very specific way, inform his daily life ... and then how he might triumph over this. Because I think that in any story – certainly in any mythic fable, which is what we're making – you want to move the character forward."

Left: Robin on the rocky shore of the Riddler's Claw Island. *Inset:* Dick Grayson tools around with one of Bruce Wayne's classic motorcycles. *Right:* Batman scales a balcony at the Nygmatech party with the help of his Bat Grapple Hook.

"So with that in mind, Joel and I looked to see where Bruce Wayne would begin psychologically, and then where he would move to. We've tried to work in a new way with the other familiar characters as well. It's common now in comic books to be revisionist about the histories of the characters, and I think that's great fun. One needs to be, I think, true to the spirit of the character while using perhaps a more modern sensibility to revisit and then renew our understanding of that character. I think we've done that with Edward Nygma/the Riddler, and also Harvey Dent, who becomes Two-Face ... and obviously with Robin."

Creating a cogent new interpretation of Robin was a great challenge for Schumacher and Goldsman, who both fully recognized the character's somewhat checkered past in the hearts of Batman fans.

"Dick Grayson is really a very interesting character," says the screenwriter, "one of the most maligned characters in the Batman series. Robin is killed over and over again in the comic books, in his various identities. But the truest and purest Robin, I think, will always be Dick Grayson. Here is a young man whose tragedy very clearly echoes young Bruce Wayne's, and again, we tried to make that emotional scenario more authentic to both characters while keeping the heightened comedy, drama and fun of the comic books."

Schumacher decided to age Dick Grayson somewhat from previous versions of the story, feeling that this would create a more interesting big brother/little brother relationship between Bruce and Dick, rather than have the older man serve as a more conventional parental figure to his "ward." (Indeed, it's really Alfred who is surrogate father to them both).

Newly invented for *Batman Forever* is Dr. Chase Meridian, who works in the field of mental health as a well-known psychiatrist specializing in dual personalities. "Chase provides us with an intelligent insight into the workings of the other characters," explains Goldsman. "And additionally, she's stunningly gorgeous, definitely has her own personal duality, and is a great romantic match for both Batman and Bruce Wayne."

With all the characters in place, the next step was for Joel Schumacher to find the perfect actors to actually inhabit those vivid personalities. And he was just the right man to do it.

If you ask Joel Schumacher, much of what makes a movie successful begins with the casting process. Schumacher is noted for his pinpoint accuracy in spotting talent and then doing something extraordinary with it.

casting

new blood in gotham

Batman Forever presented a rich opportunity for Schumacher to cast roles that cried out for fearless, audacious and even outrageous performers.

The greatest challenge for Schumacher, of course, was to find the actor who would don the cowl and cape as the immortal title character. When Michael Keaton parted ways with the role, Schumacher knew whom he wanted to breathe new life into the Dark Knight: Val Kilmer, one of the most dedicated and versatile young leading men in American cinema.

"I had been a fan of Val since *Top Gun* and *Willow*," says Joel Schumacher. "He was incredible as Jim Morrison in *The Doors* and recently he just blew me away in *Tombstone*."

What makes Kilmer such a perfect fit for Batman? "First of all," says the director, "he's a great actor. He's extremely handsome and has a bearing which can make you believe him as Bruce Wayne, who is a charming millionaire entrepreneur and social star of Gotham ... with a secret. As Batman, Val is heroic and sexy. There's also a tremendous amount of depth, sensitivity and mystery to Val ... all qualities tailor-made for the role."

The first actor to be cast in *Batman Forever* was actually Academy Award-winner Tommy Lee Jones for the role of Two-Face.™ Conveniently, Schumacher was working with Jones at the time on location for his film *The Client*, in which the actor was starring as

the "Reverend" Roy Foltrigg. "Tommy Lee was always my first choice for Two-Face," says Schumacher, "and I asked him very early on. There's nobody like Tommy Lee Jones. I mean, who else can be this wicked, funny and daring at the same time?"

For the Riddler, one face kept appearing and reappearing in Schumacher's imagination ... Jim Carrey. "I think Jim was *born* to play this role," declares the director. "It seems so natural that I can't believe our luck. Because Jim is so brilliantly funny, there's a tendency to ignore the fact that he is a fine actor. He's enormously gifted."

Chase Meridian was, without question, one of the most sought-after female roles of the year in Hollywood.

> "I think Jim was *born* to play this role. It seems so natural that I can't believe our luck."

"I wanted Nicole Kidman from the very beginning," declares Schumacher. "She was in Canada making a film, so we couldn't meet for a long time. I've been a fan of Nicole's since *Dead Calm* and knew she would be perfect for Chase. She's a great actress who is talented, beautiful and has a terrific sense of humor."

Casting Dick Grayson/Robin was another challenge for Schumacher, who had to deal over 50 years' worth of expectations of who Robin *is*. Schumacher defied the stereotypes by casting the talented Chris O'Donnell, who is in his early 20s. States the director, "I didn't want to have an adolescent Robin. I didn't want to do a wide-eyed, cutesy, overly innocent Robin. Nor did I want an overly hip, street Robin. I wanted somebody that you believe is a young man of integrity, with

Left: Jim Carrey manipulates the Riddler's trademark question mark-tipped cane with dancer-like dexterity. *Right:* Alfred prepares the all-new Batmobile to allow the Dark Knight to make a quick exit from the Batcave.

vengeance on his mind, who would be a formidable foe with martial arts and acrobatic skills. And I wanted somebody you believe would be an acceptable partner for Batman, not some 'Holy Bat Mackerel' form of Robin.

"Chris O'Donnell has demonstrated his range both as an actor and a physical performer in his previous films," adds Schumacher, "and I hope people will be as excited as we are to have him in the movie."

Also featured in the new cast are Drew Barrymore and Debi Mazar, who portray Two-Face's "luscious" gun molls, Sugar and Spice. "Drew and Debi are equally talented, beautiful, clever and funny," says Schumacher, "and the roles are a lot of fun."

Schumacher decided to maintain tradition by bringing back two distinguished veterans of both *Batman* and *Batman Returns,* as Michael Gough and Pat Hingle recreated their respective roles of Alfred and Police Commissioner Gordon. Explains the director, "Michael and Pat are two great actors, and they created these roles. The idea of changing them just for the sake of changing them would have been, I think, a mistake. We already had a wonderful Alfred and Commissioner Gordon ... and so they remained."

ready to rock
... and roll

The cast was set. After five months of pre-production, all the departments were ready to roll.

The actors were certainly anxious to get in front of the cameras. At a costume and makeup test filmed a week before principal photography, Jim Carrey (in Riddler regalia) practiced in the wings like a devilish Astaire, relentlessly developing character and nuance, manipulating the Riddler's trademark question mark-tipped gold cane with the aplomb of a world champion baton twirler.

Meanwhile, Joel Schumacher, Peter Macgregor-Scott and others were watching mechanical effects supervisor Tommy Fisher fire up the revamped Batmobile for the first time. They were awestruck. "Val, have you seen it?," Schumacher excitedly asked the new Batman.

To which Kilmer humorously replied – in character – "Have I seen it? I *built* it!" Kilmer then turned his head and called out, "Alfred ... get me a wrench!"

It was *definitely* time for this movie to start shooting!

THE CAST
what's new in gotham

Burbank, California. Michael Keaton has decided not to return to the role of Batman, and there are important discussions at Warner Bros. as to who will be the next Dark Knight – one of the most sought-after parts in American cinema. Again and again, one name is mentioned by director Joel Schumacher . . .

Cut to the Kalahari Desert, Southern Africa. A young actor is on a research trip for a future film project he's writing. He's sleeping in the bush and has been out of contact with Hollywood for five weeks. Spiritually, he's more attuned to the lives of the Kalahari bushmen and the natural world that surrounds him than to the daily buzz of the film industry.

Some time later, when he lands in London, the actor's wife informs him at the hotel that a couple of faxes

val kilmer
BATMAN

just arrived ... including one that says "Congratulations, you're Batman."

Val Kilmer realizes that at the approximate moment in time that casting decision had been made, he was in a cave full of bats in the wilderness of South Africa . . .

So is Val Kilmer a believer in synchronicity?

"Yes," he replies. "I'd already begun my preparation for the Dark Knight."

Perhaps that is the key to the entire career of this remarkable actor. Kilmer's brilliant performances have synthesized research and intuition, resulting in roles that have radiated physicality and intellect. The chameleon-like Kilmer has inhabited a wide range of roles so completely that he's virtually unrecognizable from film to film. But he also has the charismatic, devastatingly handsome looks that mark a classic movie star.

Batman is not the first fabled figure that Val Kilmer has portrayed on screen. From music legends like Jim Morrison (*The Doors*) and Elvis Presley (*True Romance*) to Wild West legends like Doc Holliday (*Tombstone*) and Billy the Kid (*Gore Vidal's Billy the Kid*), Kilmer is no stranger to larger-than-life acting roles. However, he's managed to find the humanity in each of them, and never more so than in *Batman Forever*, which explores the events and inner struggles that metamorphosed Bruce Wayne into Gotham City's guardian of the night.

Left and above: Val Kilmer plays the dual roles of Batman and Bruce Wayne with studied concentration and great elan.

Classical acting training, combined with extensive experience, has enabled Kilmer to shine in compelling, eclectic roles. He was the youngest student ever admitted into the dramatic department of the prestigious Juilliard School in New York City, where he starred in *Electra and Orestes*, *Richard III* and *Macbeth*.

After making his feature film debut in the 1984 comedy *Top Secret!*, Kilmer rose to cinematic fame as Iceman, the "best of the best," opposite Tom Cruise in the blockbuster, *Top Gun*. Kilmer then took the role of the

"It was really a perfect kind of job, but one that you can never plan or want"

adventurer Madmartigan, in the fantasy epic *Willow*.

Following John Dahl's cult noir film *Kill Me Again*, Kilmer was cast by Oliver Stone to reincarnate rock star/poet Jim Morrison in *The Doors*. The role, for which Kilmer did all of his own singing in the live concert sequences, won high praise from critics and audiences for the actor's total immersion in a very demanding project.

Combining his career with his social conscience, Kilmer starred in Michael Apted's political drama, *Thunderheart*. After reuniting with Top Gun director Tony Scott for his role as Elvis in *True Romance*, Kilmer then received extensive critical praise for his portrayal of Doc Holliday in the 1993 hit *Tombstone*.

After completing Jean-Jacques Annaud's IMAX 3-D epic *Wings of Courage*, Kilmer played an unconventional

Left: Batman climbs into the Riddler's lair.
Above: Bruce Wayne confers with his head
of personnel and Commissioner Gordon
(right) after Fred Stickley's sudden demise.

psychiatrist opposite Anne Parillaud in
the offbeat *Dead Girl.* Immediately following his work on *Batman Forever,* the
energetic Kilmer segued into a starring
role with Robert De Niro and Al Pacino in
Warner Bros.' *Heat.*

Throughout his career, Kilmer has
appeared in a wide variety of stage productions. He made his Broadway debut
in the 1983 production of *Slab Boys,* and
appeared in the title role of Hamlet for the
Colorado Shakespeare Festival. He most
recently starred in *'Tis Pity She's A Whore*
in New York.

On television, Kilmer starred in sev-
eral highly regarded TV movies, including
HBO's *The Man Who Broke A Thousand
Chains* – for which he received an ACE
Award nomination – and *Gore Vidal's Billy
the Kid* for TNT.

When he stepped off that plane
from Africa, Kilmer was more than a little
pleased to learn that he had won the role
of Batman from his wife, actress Joanne
Whalley-Kilmer, who had just completed
six months of work as another figure of
legendary Americana – Scarlett O'Hara –
in the mini-series *Scarlett.* But Kilmer
never thought that it was destiny for him

to play the part. "It is an extraordinary opportunity, but one that you could never plan," says Kilmer. "The circumstances were all so strange anyway, since Batman is such a substantial character and the two other films were so successful, and Michael Keaton was so good. I never thought, 'They're going to do a third Batman film and I wonder if they're going to recast it.' It was just a happy series of bizarre circumstances."

The 100-day-plus shoot – and the need to wear a 40 pound Batsuit – presented Kilmer with circumstances that would tax the healthiest of actors. But Kilmer is no stranger to such challenges. "I've done jobs that were longer," he notes. "*Willow* had an almost six month-long shooting schedule, six-day weeks in three different countries. Hamlet talks for two-and-a-half straight hours if you collect all his dialogue. That is demanding. I tend to pick jobs that way."

Kilmer's not sure if he actively seeks out such extreme working conditions, but admits that "I really like character-driven parts on sets where everything is stylized, like westerns. That's really a genre I love, because I own horses, and grew up spending a lot of time in Arizona, New Mexico and the Western states. My father was raised on Indian land in New Mexico. Actually, I would do a bad western with a good horse any day of the week."

Certainly, *Batman Forever* fits the Kilmer bill of a character-driven part on sets where everything is stylized, and the actor obviously did his homework. "The character has been a major force in comic books since 1939 and is still a mammoth business," notes Kilmer. "That means there's obviously something fascinating and of primal interest to audiences. The Batman comics deal with the gray area in between good and evil. He's not always on steady ground with the community. Batman's compulsion is to extract justice at night, but he also has a real sense of irony, in a wonderful comedic style that Bob Kane invented."

When it's mentioned that Batman is, after all, a vigilante, Kilmer notes "but so is (American consumer rights advocate) Ralph Nader. By living out his principles that are very personal, Nader has affected the whole globe. I think Batman is distinctly American in that sense. We are a radical nation, and I think that Batman would probably not be very successful if he decided that he would become Batcounselor and talk to villains instead of fighting them."

> **"The Batman comics deal with the gray area in between good and evil. He's not always on steady ground with the community."**

Kilmer is an activist of a more peaceable kind than his on-screen character, an ardent supporter of Native American affairs and an advocate of environmental protection. He supports Lead or Leave, a non-partisan, youth political awareness campaign, and Habitat for Humanity, an organization that raises money to construct houses for low-income families.

And although Kilmer portrays the ultimate urbanite in *Batman Forever*, he lives with wife Joanne Whalley-Kilmer and their daughter in rural New Mexico, close to the open Southwest landscape that he felt so close to as a youngster.

On the set, Kilmer brought a wry, dry sense of humor, great charm as Bruce Wayne and intense concentration when in costume as the Dark Knight. And somewhere beyond the 80th day of filming, as the schedule wended its way toward completion, the actor observed – with characteristic wit and honest insight – "It's not a job. It's a lifestyle!" Incidentally, *Batman Forever* did *not* mark the first time Val Kilmer sat in the driver's seat of the Batmobile. When he was in first grade, Kilmer's mother took the lucky lad to the set of the ABC-TV series at the invitation of a friend who was working in the special effects department. The biggest thrill of all for the young Val was being allowed to sit in the cockpit of George Barris' long, black, bubble-domed Batmobile.

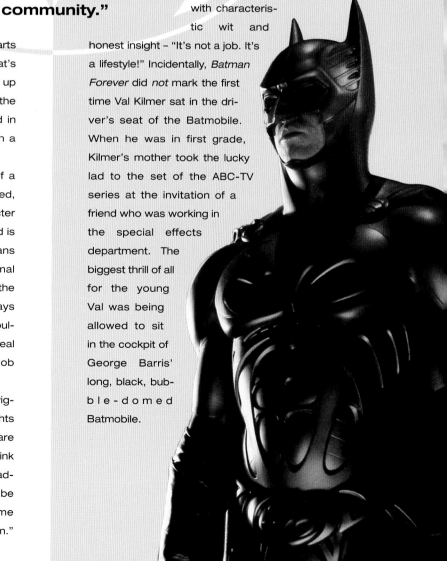

The degree of concentration and dedication that Tommy Lee Jones brings to each and every one of his screen performances can be witnessed to amazing advantage in *Batman Forever*, Scene 40. In this sequence, Two-Face and his thugs have invaded the Second Bank of Gotham, and the double-your displeasure villain, who is standing with his back to the window, growls "Let's start this party with a bang."

tommy lee jones
Two-Face

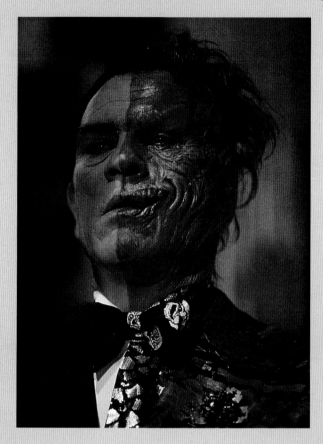

level of stardom, culminating in a 1993 Academy Award for Best Supporting Actor for his portrayal of a relentless FBI agent pursuing Harrison Ford in *The Fugitive*. But the straight-talking Texan made his sentiments quite clear in his acceptance speech when he said, "I'm lucky enough to be working." And audiences could certainly appreciate his statement, as there are few performers that are so magnetic on screen.

Jones was the first actor summoned by the director Joel Schumacher to join the cast of *Batman Forever*, which was made convenient by the fact that they were working together at the time in the

"With *Batman Forever* we're living in a world of comic books, not the world of great American literature. Two-Face is a simple bifurcated character, Jekyll and Hyde simplified to the cartoon level."

At that moment, a giant wrecking ball smashes through the wall and into the vault room, inches away from smashing Two-Face as well.

Filmed on Warner Bros. Stage 16, Jones insisted on doing this stunt himself, and he played the scene utterly unfazed by the flames, loud explosion, sputtering sparks and humongous iron ball that might have taken out one of Hollywood's finest actors – had that actor flinched or accidentally stepped in the wrong direction. But for Tommy Lee Jones, it's another day of work in a profession that he loves.

Ask anyone in the motion picture business, and they will likely confirm that Tommy Lee Jones defines the word "actor." Having made his big screen debut nearly 25 years ago, Jones' tremendous range has always been noted by audiences and critics. But it's been in the past few years that Jones has finally achieved a fitting

Deep South filming *The Client*. Schumacher knew that Jones would achieve his usual on-screen perfection as the first actor ever to portray Batman's legendary arch-villain Two-Face, also known as Gotham District Attorney Harvey Dent.

Between the winning of his Best Supporting Actor Oscar for *The Fugitive* and the release of *Batman Forever*, Jones was seen in five other films, starring opposite Jeff Bridges in *Blown Away*, Susan Sarandon in *The Client*, Jessica Lange in *Blue Sky*, portraying a mad prison warden in Oliver Stone's *Natural Born Killers* and the title role in Ron Shelton's *Cobb*, about the legendary baseball player.

As if that extraordinary stretch of non-stop work wasn't enough, Jones also made his debut as a director on the Turner Network TV presentation of *The Good Old Boys*, writing the screenplay as well as starring (with Sissy Spacek and Sam Shepard) in the adaptation of Elmer Kelton's novel.

Following such a prolific stretch of dramatic roles, Jones was attracted to the notion of portraying a character rooted in the realm of the fantastic.

"With *Batman Forever* we're living in a world of comic books," notes Jones, "not the world of great American literature. Two-Face is a simple bifurcated character, Jekyll and Hyde simplified to the cartoon level. When I met Bob Kane, I asked him if that's what he had in mind when he created Two-Face, and he said yes to that question."

Throughout the myriad versions of Batman in all media, Two-Face is a character who has until now remained untouched by live-action interpretation ... even in the 1960s television series, which utilized so many of the comic book Gotham City villains that new ones had to be invented. "Maybe they thought it was a bit tough," suggests Jones, "or hard to look at for the '60s TV screen. They didn't have the makeup capabilities that we have today. It may have been just the degree of difficulty."

Below: Two-Face with his "bad" moll Spice, reflecting the darker side of his nature. *Right:* The Riddler and Two-Face admire a precious gem which they're about to steal from a jewelry store.

Jones has never been intimidated by the degree of difficulty in any of his roles, emerging triumphantly with some of the silver screen's most memorable performances. He received his first Academy Award nomination in 1991, portraying the effete, aristocratic, sinister Clay Shaw in Oliver Stone's *JFK*. Jones was also nominated for a Golden Globe for *JFK* and later received that award for *The Fugitive*. Jones' first Golden Globe nomination came for *Coal Miner's Daughter* in 1980, in which he portrayed country star Loretta Lynn's hard-living husband.

After graduating *cum laude* from Harvard University with a degree in English literature, Jones moved to New York, where he made his Broadway debut in John Osborne's *A Patriot for Me*. His other Broadway appearances included *Four in a Garden* with Carol Channing and Sid Caesar, and *Ulysses in Nighttown* with the late Zero Mostel.

Jones made his film debut in Arthur Hiller's *Love Story* (1970) as Ryan O'Neal's roommate. Subsequent features have included *Jackson County Jail*, *Rolling Thunder*, *Eyes of Laura Mars*, *The River Rats*, *Stormy Monday*, *The Package*, *Fire Birds*, *House of Cards*, the smash action hit *Under Siege* and a powerful perfor-

Above: Two-Face takes careful aim at Bruce Wayne in Wayne Manor.
Right: The Riddler gives the mesmerized Two-Face a taste of the Box, his brain-draining invention.

Rainmaker for HBO, the HBO/BBC production of *Yuri Nosenko, KGB* and *April Morning*.

A native of San Saba, Texas, Jones and his wife Kimberlea still live in the Lone Star State with their two children.

Along with all his hard work comes abundant recompense. "It's been a lot of fun," says Jones of his *Batman Forever* experience. "I've known Joel Schumacher for twenty years and I've done two movies with him. Ve Neill and Eddie Henriques are doing the makeup, and they've been old pals for a long time. And I love working for Warner Bros. I hope it doesn't sound specious to refer to

"I like the scale of this movie, which is, on the scale of things, huge. If a movie gets bigger than this, it's a mistake, and this is not a mistake. We're doing all this on purpose. It's Batman, after all."

mance as a psychologically wounded Vietnam veteran in Oliver Stone's *Heaven and Earth.*

On television, Jones won an Emmy Award in 1982 for Best Actor for his portrayal of condemned killer Gary Gilmore in the mini-series *The Executioner's Song*, adapted by Norman Mailer from his book. He received both Emmy and Golden Globe Award nominations in 1989 for his role in the acclaimed mini-series *Lonesome Dove*, based on the Pulitzer Prize-winning novel about the Wild West by Larry McMurtry. Jones' other TV credits have included the title role in *The Amazing Howard Hughes*, the American Playhouse production of *Cat on a Hot Tin Roof*, *The*

a giant corporation like Warner Bros. as family, but they are one.

"I also like the scale of this movie," concludes Jones, "which is, on the scale of things, huge. If a movie gets bigger than this, it's a mistake, and this is not a mistake. We're doing all this on purpose. It's Batman, after all. What further explanation could one possibly want? It's a mountain you want to climb because it's there."

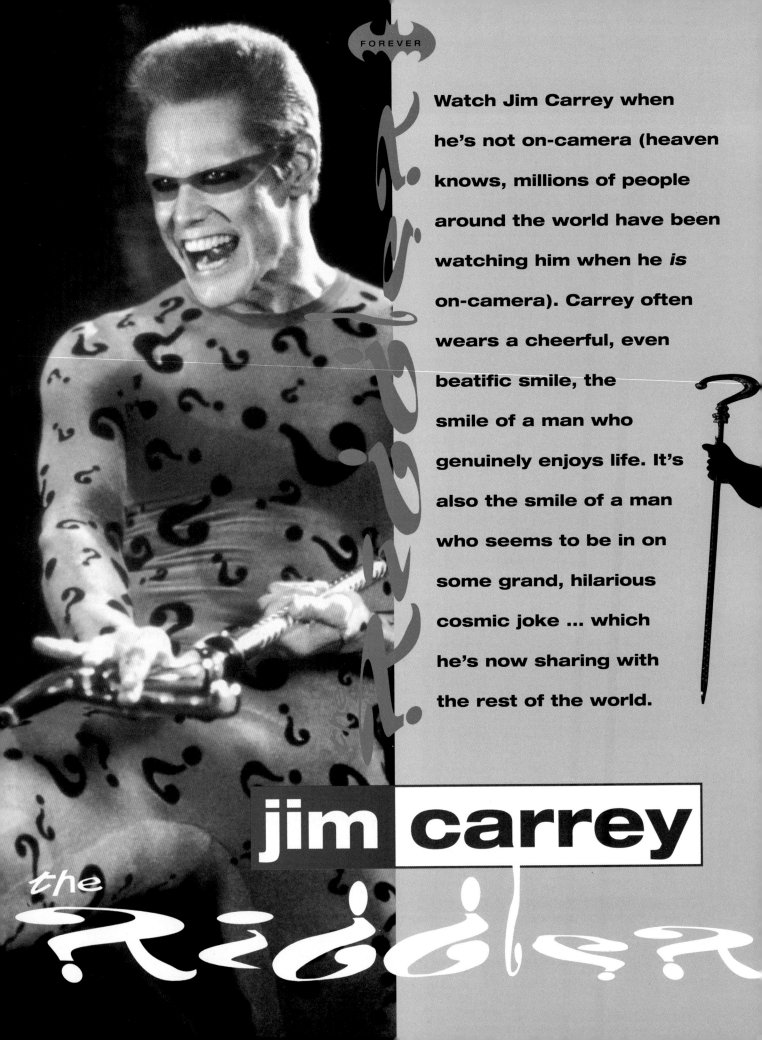

What a phenomenal year 1994 was for Jim Carrey: He starred in not one, not two, but three films – *Ace Ventura: Pet Detective*, *The Mask* and *Dumb and Dumber* – which collectively grossed more than $400-million worldwide! If laughter is truly an international language, then Carrey has smacked the entire world on the funnybone. The bottom line is that people love Jim Carrey for a rather simple reason: He makes them laugh, in big, guffawing, side-splitting, roll-'em-in-the-aisles style.

Carrey combines the physical genius of the top silent-screen comics with the verbal dexterity of a post-modern performance artist. Gifted with a body of unbelievable flexibility – which he utilizes with the aplomb of a Baryshnikov gone happily berserk – Carrey has created a gallery of delightfully bizarre characters in movies and on television that nearly defy description.

The latest feath-

er tickling Carrey's cap is his performance as Edward Nygma and his more malevolent manifestation, the Riddler, in *Batman Forever*.

It seems that Carrey was born to play this role, but when he heard the news of his own casting, he wasn't exactly blasé. "I was so excited I was out of my mind," he admits. "I was at the Cannes Film Festival promoting *The Mask*, and I was standing on the balcony of my hotel watching people flock around Gerard Depardieu.

Opposite: Coral hair ablaze, the Riddler uses his signature question-mark cane to great effect. *Above:* Another guise for Jim Carrey as the Riddler. *Above right:* Super-nerd Ed Nygma disposes of his boss, Fred Stickley (Ed Begley Jr.) by pushing him through the window.

Somebody came in and told me that they wanted me to do the Riddler, which was like the icing on the cake.

"I was excited to have the chance to work with a really experienced director like Joel Schumacher, and I didn't even realize that I was standing on the balcony in my bathrobe, with everybody looking up at me from down below!"

Carrey was intrigued at the challenge of playing Edward Nygma, who actually mutates into several different versions of both himself and his criminal alter-ego, the Riddler. "Even when Edward starts out at the beginning of the story," explains Carrey, "he's already pretty much gone, psychologically speaking. I like the sycophantic, stalker aspect of the character, the way Edward worships Bruce Wayne. When Edward finally meets Bruce, it's supposed to be like John the Baptist meeting Jesus, but it doesn't turn out that way. Sycophants and stalkers already hate and resent the person they idolize, so Edward turns against Bruce with a fury."

The role gave Carrey numerous opportunities to give full demonstrations of his incredible physicality,

particularly his miraculous twirling of the Riddler's signature gold cane.

"You wouldn't think it was so miraculous if you came to my house and saw all the dents in the wall!" responds Carrey.

In fact, Carrey worked on the cane twirling with the great comic actor David Shiner, who showed him the basic moves. After that, the cane was almost never out of Carrey's hands, either at home or on the set between takes. "You know, if you want to learn how to throw a football, you just sleep with the darn thing," notes Carrey.

"The cane really did become a part of me. Weird."

In fact, Batman was a part of Carrey's life as a kid in Newmarket, Ontario, Canada, where he was born on January 17, 1962. "The routine was," Carrey recalls, "watch the *Batman* TV show at 7:30, then wash your face, neck, arms, hands and go to bed. Or no, it was the other way around. If I *didn't* wash my face, neck, arms and hands, I couldn't watch *Batman*."

So in effect, Batman kept Jim Carrey a clean young man. But he had other things on his mind. By age three, Carrey was already a class clown, and he knew that show

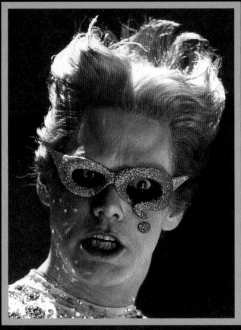

Miain picture: The Riddler manically rejoices in the mayhem and destruction he has wrought in the Batcave. *Far left:* Jim Carrey as Edward Nygma, extolling the virtues of his new invention – the Box. *Left:* One of the Riddler's more bizarre costumes.

starring roles in Francis Coppola's *Peggy Sue Got Married, Earth Girls Are Easy* and *The Dead Pool.*

Carrey's first Showtime comedy special, *Jim Carrey's Unnatural Act,* premiered in 1991 to rave reviews. He also starred in the TV movie *Doing Time on Maple Drive.*

As soon as he became a regular performer on the weekly ensemble comedy hit, *In Living Color,* Carrey's huge range of abilities was exposed to the American public on a grand scale. It was only a matter of time before he would once again be cast in a feature film starring role, which soon occurred with Carrey's no-holds-barred portrayal of *Ace Ventura: Pet Detective.* The "overnight success" of Jim Carrey had finally taken place ... nearly 15 years after arriving in the City of Angels!

Through it all, that remarkably innocent smile has remained on Jim Carrey's face. "You can't take this too seriously," he says. "I mean, if you really start thinking about it, the money and stuff, it would freak you out. You wouldn't be able to be creative. I don't wake up thinking about money. It's still playtime for me."

One example of playtime was the day that Carrey, as the Riddler, gleefully blew the Batcave to smithereens with his little, green Batty Bombs. The actor betrayed no fear whatsoever as the flames and sparks wildly shot around the giant set. After the biggest explosion – with flames to the left, right and rear of Carrey – director Joel Schumacher asked with concern, "Are you okay, Jim?" Utterly nonplussed, Carrey the perfectionist responded, "Sure ... but can we do it again?"

And they did!

> **"Even when Edward starts out at the beginning of the story, he's already pretty much *gone*, psychologically speaking. I like the sycophantic, stalker aspect of the character, the way Edward worships Bruce Wayne."**

business was in the cards. At age 15, he took off for Toronto to perform at Yuk Yuks, the famous comedy club. After a bumpy start, his career took off and for the next couple of years, he worked all over Canada. By age 19, he had gone as far as he could and needed to spread his wings; so in 1981 he packed his belongings and moved to Los Angeles.

Carrey immediately became a regular at Mitzi Shore's Comedy Store, and a year later MTM cast him as the star of their NBC series, *Duck Factory.* In 1984 he starred in his first feature, *Once Bitten,* followed by co-

Every one of the five major characters in _Batman Forever_ wears two very different sets of clothing, and each has two complete and separate identities and names ... except Dr. Chase Meridian, the exceptionally brilliant and beautiful police psychiatrist who specializes in dual personalities.

On the other hand ... while Chase doesn't change her name, or don a cape and mask, she too alters her personality when the Gotham moon appears and when the lure of the night leads her into a more shadowy side of her soul. To imbue this character with a full on-screen life, Joel Schumacher chose a star who serves up prodigious acting skills and astonishing beauty in equal measures ... Nicole Kidman.

"Chase is attracted to the dark side of life," says Kidman, "and that's why Batman is so appealing to her. She's always been that way, as she explains in the movie, but she wants to examine and deal with that part of herself, which is what she does during the course of the film."

Nicole Kidman was a major movie star before she

nicole kidman

Dr. Chase Meridian

ever left Australia to do an American film. She made her screen debut at the age of 14 in the Australian picture, *Bush Christmas*, and then starred in a number of productions Down Under, including *Winners*, *Dead Calm*, *Emerald City* (for which she received a Best Supporting Actress nomination from the Australian Film Institute) and *Flirting*. She also starred in the television mini-series *Five-Mile Creek*, *Vietnam* (which made Kidman an overnight star at 17) and *Bangkok Hilton*, the last two garnering the actress several Australian awards.

It wasn't long before the American film industry noticed Kidman's sterling qualities. She traveled to the U.S. and soon after her arrival secured the starring role opposite Tom Cruise in *Days of Thunder*.

Since then, Kidman has enjoyed non-stop success as one of the most sought-after stars in the industry, toplining in *Billy Bathgate*, the epic *Far and Away*, *My Life* and *Malice*. Just

Above: The Riddler prepares to knock Chase Meridian out with a nasty injection. *Right:* Chase, held prisoner in the Riddler's Lair. *Inset:* Chase Meridian, revealing the aggressive side of her nature, works out on the punchbag in her office.

prior to beginning her work in *Batman Forever*, Kidman starred in Gus Van Sant's black comedy, *2 Die 4*, and is currently set to play the title role in the film version of the Henry James novel, *Portrait of a Lady*.

In *Batman Forever*, Chase is in love with Batman, but she is pursued by Bruce Wayne. She initially sees Bruce as the "safer" choice, making him less interesting than the man in the jet-black cape. "I like the twist in the triangle," says Kidman, "and one of my favorite scenes is when I'm kissing Batman and realizing that I'm in love with Bruce Wayne. There's comedic material that's also quite touching."

> **"Chase is attracted to the dark side of life and that's why Batman is so appealing to her"**

Kidman had already proven herself to be game for physically demanding roles in *Dead Calm* and *Far and Away*, and Chase Meridian is similarly a character who often expresses herself in a uniquely active manner. That includes knocking the daylights out of a punching bag in her office when she first encounters Bruce Wayne, and later in the story, she handily dispatches some of Two-Face's thugs in Wayne Manor. "I'm learning kickboxing," says Kidman, "because it's such an interesting sport now for women. I thought that would be something that would give another twist to Chase's personality."

"My biggest goal as an actress is to be versatile," concludes Kidman. "What I admire the most is the ability to play all sorts of roles and not get pigeonholed. I like to mix it up!"

It has been almost 30 years since Robin has been portrayed by a live actor, but Chris O'Donnell rose to the challenge with his usual infectious blend of humility, confidence and easy physicality.

In his early 20s, and already a veteran of a number of highly successful films, the Chicago born-and-based O'Donnell was more than ready to attack this superhero-sized character. He had already played a period action-adventure hero in the Disney remake of *The Three Musketeers* as the dashing young swordsman D'Artagnan.

O'Donnell is a bonafide Batman fan who still owns his tie-in toys from the 1960s TV series. "I thought the opportunity to play a character that I'd grown up watching was really exciting," says O'Donnell. He was shooting *Mad Love*, a road movie with Drew Barrymore, when the call came from Joel Schumacher. "I was so busy that it didn't really sink in," admits the young actor.

It became more of a reality later, when Schumacher and stunt coordinator Conrad Palmisano arranged a rigorous physical training program for O'Donnell that included martial arts and studying trapeze. As in Bob Kane's original comic book, the Dick Grayson of *Batman Forever* is a talented circus acrobat, which meant that O'Donnell had to

chris o'donnell
ROBIN

become a more-than-proficient man on the flying trapeze. "It was a little scary at first," says O'Donnell, "because you can't believe that you're actually up there. But it wasn't bad. When I worked on *The Three Musketeers* I had to learn horseback riding, fencing and gymnastics."

O'Donnell's Dick Grayson/Robin portrayal is an audacious creation which incorporates elements of the character familiar to generations of Batman fans ... but with a '90s edge. Not quite the squeaky clean all-American boy of the *Batman* TV show, O'Donnell's Dick Grayson is the kind of young man you would expect to emerge from a life as a traveling circus performer. "The image I always had in my head was something that Joel had said earlier on," notes O'Donnell. "Dick and his family lived in a gypsy lifestyle, unconventional and unpre-

> **"Joel Schumacher has the most easygoing set that I've ever been on. It's like I'm getting paid to play around the way I did when I was a little kid."**

Supporting Actor – four Academy Award nominations (with Pacino winning as Best Actor) and the Chicago Film Critics Award for O'Donnell as Most Promising Actor of the Year. He went on to star in *The Three Musketeers*, for which he was named the NATO/ShoWest Male Star of Tomorrow for 1994.

O'Donnell bounded into *Batman Forever* on the heels of two other movies, the period romantic comedy *Circle of Friends*, shot in Ireland, and the more contemporary dramatic love story, *Mad Love*.

The irrepressible O'Donnell endeared himself to all as a wise-cracking whirlwind who is quick with a quip, but absolutely dedicated to the task at hand. And he responded enthusiastically to the on-set atmosphere created by the film's director: "Joel Schumacher has the most easygoing set that I've ever been on," notes O'Donnell. "It's like I'm getting paid to play around the way I did when I was a little kid, with friends coming over and having battles in the basement."

Did O'Donnell ever envision himself starring in a Batman movie while watching the series as a kid?

"Oh yeah," he responds. "But I don't know if I made believe that I was Robin ... I think I probably made believe that I was Batman!"

Far left: Chris O'Donnell as Robin in the "high-tech" suit. *Left:* The crew prepares O'Donnell for a stunt in Wayne Manor. *Below:* Dick Grayson takes a tumble in his attempt to spy out the secrets of Bruce Wayne's mansion.

dictable. That's why we went for a subtle gypsy look."

Chris O'Donnell is the youngest of seven children from a Chicago suburb, where he still makes his home. He first came to prominence when he was cast, at the age of 17, as Jessica Lange's rebellious teenage son in *Men Don't Leave*. O'Donnell followed with well-received roles in *Blue Sky*, *School Ties* and a memorable cameo in *Fried Green Tomatoes*.

In 1992, O'Donnell starred opposite Al Pacino in *Scent of a Woman*, which received five Golden Globe nominations – including one for O'Donnell as Best

Although the elegant and distinguished Michael Gough embodied Alfred in both *Batman* and *Batman Returns*, he came to the third film with no dimming of enthusiasm or eagerness to expand the role. Quite the contrary ... Gough's energy level would shame many a man a fraction of his age, and he was anxious to slip back into Alfred's formal black jacket and white collar.

"I feel very confident with Alfred," says Gough, "because he is such a straightforward, unequivocal character." However, the actor notes that for *Batman Forever*, director Schumacher and writer Akiva Goldsman sought to further examine the profound, surrogate father/son relationship between Alfred and Bruce Wayne.

"The difference really is not so much in Alfred himself," continues Gough, "but in his relationship to Batman and Bruce Wayne. Playing a scene with Michael Keaton was inevitably different than playing a scene with Val Kilmer, because they're two different actors. Luckily,

> **"I was blessed to have worked with Val in *Top Secret!*, so he was already a friend and we already had a working and personal relationship, which made acting with a new Batman and Bruce much easier."**

I was blessed to have worked with Val in *Top Secret!*, so he was already a friend and we already had a working and personal relationship, which made acting with a new Batman and Bruce much easier." Gough points out that the way in which Alfred relates to Bruce/Batman changes according circumstance. "If Batman is in trouble, then Alfred has to be the father. If Batman is bravely going out like a hero against the world, then I've got to stand by as both colleague and nurse, in case he gets hurt. And other times I've got to be the servant. But always the servant with dignity ... never the servile servant!"

In *Batman Forever*, Alfred is seen to greater advantage in his role. "Scriptwise, there's a difference in what Alfred does," says Gough about the new film, "but his internal workings are just the same. And happily, Joel Schumacher allows me to be free to perform the way I'm comfortable. Joel is a miracle man, as far as directors go. He's entirely sympathetic, but won't let anything go that he doesn't like. He really wants you to be good, and he likes actors."

michael gough
Alfred

The wittily self-deprecating Gough made his first stage appearance with London's Old Vic theatre company in 1936, this Malayan-born son of a British rubber planter has appeared in more than 50 films, from the sublime (*Anna Karenina*, *The Man in the White Suit*, *Richard III*, *The Go-Between*, *The Dresser*, *Out of Africa*, *Caravaggio*, *Strapless* and *The Age of Innocence*) to the marvelously ridiculous (a series of horror films that have included *Horror of Dracula*, *Konga*, *The Phantom of the Opera*, *Black Zoo*, *Berserk!*, *The Skull* and *Trog*).

Still Gough regrets nothing in his magnificent career. "I am not, and never could be a star," he claimed. "It's something that has never concerned me, or remotely interested me. I want to work and keep on working. I do not want to become a commodity, and thank God, I never have. I have been very, very lucky."

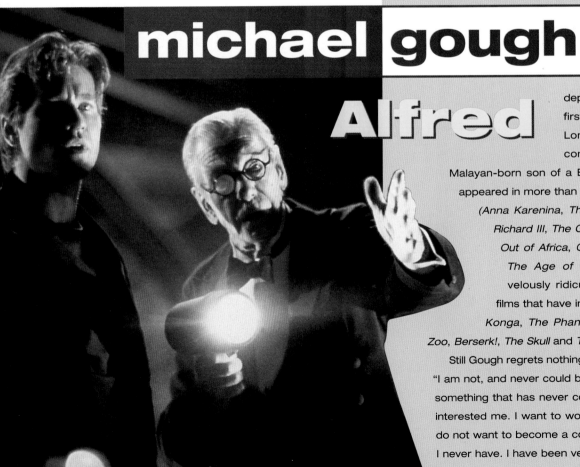

When the time came to cast Gotham's endlessly belea-guered Commissioner Gordon in *Batman Forever*, Schumacher knew whom to summon. "Pat Hingle cannot do a bad take," notes Schumacher, and plenty of other directors must agree with that summation, since Hingle has worked non-stop in all media for more than 40 years.

Commissioner Gordon maintains an important place in Batman lore; he's an eminently human individual des-perately trying to cope with crime in a lawless city. In *Batman Forever*, Gordon already has a history of cooper-ation with the Dark Knight, despite the fact that Batman wears no badge and has no official sanction to fight crime. Gordon not only allows Batman free access, but actually calls upon his assistance with the huge Bat-Signal mounted on the roof of the Gotham Police Headquarters.

"Batman is like a gift from heaven who sort of came into being for the Gotham Police Department," says Hingle. "When Batman first arrived in Gotham City, Gordon hardly believed that he actually existed. Now it's reached a point that when a situation comes up that Gordon and his department can't handle on their own, they throw up a Bat-Signal and there Batman comes!"

Despite hailing from the opposite side of the Atlantic from Micheal Gough, the two man have much in common. Both have huge bodies of distinguished work in theatre, movies and TV. Both are actors who have barely stopped working for their entire careers, and have left their egos at the door in pursuit of professional excellence.

Pat Hingle, hailing from Denver, Colorado, has starred in 22 Broadway plays, four of which – *J.B.*, *Cat on a Hot Tin Roof*, *Strange Interlude* and *That Championship Season* – have won Pulitzer Prizes. He made his film debut in Elia Kazan's now-classic *On the Waterfront*, and his countless screen appearances also include *Splendor in the Grass*, *No Down Payment*, *The Ugly American*, *Norma Rae*, *The Falcon and the Snowman*, *The Grifters* and *The Quick and the Dead*. With Clint Eastwood, Hingle co-starred in *Hang 'Em High*, *The Gauntlet* and *Sudden Impact*. Hingle's voluminous TV appearances have includ-ed the mini-series *LBJ: The Early Days*, *War and Remembrance* and *The Kennedys of Massachusetts*.

So what makes *Batman Forever* different for Hingle and his screen incarnation of Commissioner Gordon? "Well, in addition to having a new Batman and new arch-villains, we also have what I think a lot of people have been waiting for. Everybody keeps asking 'Where the heck is Robin?' So this time's he's going to come and help both Batman and Commissioner Gordon!"

pat hingle

Commissioner Gordon

names, Sugar is fluffy, frilly and melt-in-your mouth adorable; Spice is black-leathery, tattoo-tough and in-your-face aggressive. To exemplify these distaff mirror images, Schumacher summoned the services of two fine and alluring actresses: Drew Barrymore and Debi Mazar.

"I think that Sugar is just a very pure, angelic, evil, delicious creature," says Drew Barrymore of her character. "She represents the good side of Two-Face, but the good side of Two-Face is still evil."

Barrymore was happy to accept the offer of playing Sugar from her long-time friend Joel Schumacher, whom she had known since she was only seven years old and who had previously directed her in the television pilot *2000 Malibu Road*. "I love Joel," Barrymore says emphatically. "He's just been the kindest, most wonderful friend, and he's also the best person to work for. As a director, he's incredible to work with because he's a professional, an actor's director, and visually he puts everything completely out 100 per cent. I think that he has something unique from any other director I've ever worked with."

That's an impressive list of directors, considering the fact that the film which made Barrymore famous – at the age of six – was directed by Steven Spielberg. That's the classic *E.T. The Extra-Terrestrial*, in which young Drew charmed audiences as Gertie. More recently, Barrymore has impressed critics and audiences in such films as the 1995 Warner Bros. comedy-drama *Boys on the Side*, *Bad Girls* and *Guncrazy*, for which she received a Golden Globe nomination. Also in 1995, she was seen starring with her *Batman Forever* colleague, Chris O'Donnell, in *Mad Love*, a drama of romantic obsession.

Some things are inseparable, like coffee and donuts, cookies and milk, bread and jam ... and Sugar and Spice.

These two diametrically opposed vixens – or, as director Joel Schumacher calls them, "the ultimate party girls" – go where the action is. And during the action of *Batman Forever*, they're with the loathsome Two-Face, each of them a girlfriend of a different nature, adhering to the two sides of Two-Face's personality. Appropriate to their

drew barrymore

Sugar

On television, Barrymore starred in the title role of the ABC movie-of-the-week *The Amy Fisher Story*, which became that season's highest-rated telefeature.

Barrymore, whose first professional performance was at the age of 11 months in a dog food commercial, is the only daughter of Ildiko Jaid and John Drew Barrymore, Jr. She is descended from one of America's greatest theatrical families, with grandfather John, great-uncle Lionel and great-aunt Ethel the undisputed "Royal Family" of the American stage and screen during the first few decades of this century.

Debi Mazar grew up on the opposite end of the country from Drew Barrymore, a New York girl (and proud of it) who now lives in L.A. as well. Mazar has become increasingly in-demand by such notable directors as Oliver Stone (*The Doors*), Martin Scorsese (*Goodfellas*), Barry Levinson (*Toys*), Jodie Foster (*Little Man Tate*), Woody Allen (*Bullets Over Broadway*) and Spike Lee (*Jungle Fever*, *Malcolm X* and the recent *Clockers*). In 1995 she also stars in *Empire*, a Warner Bros. release. A TV series regular on NBC's *L.A. Law* and ABC's *Civil Wars*, she also starred in the HBO telefilm *Witch Hunt*, directed by Paul Schrader.

Mazar bit into the juicy role of Spice with characteristic relish. "It's the kind of role I've always wanted to do," she says. "I'm an avid comic book fanatic, and there's certainly a very camp side to me. So it's been a blast."

Although audiences may not agree, Mazar thinks her outrageous screen character "is very likeable. I don't know that she's necessarily so bad. She certainly has a dark side, and that's a side of me as well, which is kind of fun to throw into a character. Plus, it's so large. You can't be too over-the-top in a film like this.

"I use my body as a tool," continues Mazar, "so I went into training about two months before I started to shoot. I wanted Spice to look like a long and lean animal, but still keep it feminine. I also

had to be able to fit into the very extreme costume ... they cinched my waist in a corset down to 17 inches!"

Like Barrymore, Mazar found director Joel Schumacher open to ideas and suggestions. "Joel gave me a lot of room to play," Mazar says. "I did a lot of research in comic book stores, and out-of-print books and collections, and found these amazing 1960s super villain characters. We sat down and sketched out a lot of ideas. Joel was terrific. He's got vision, and he's completely detail-oriented."

Sugar and Spice, like sisters, are always together, but occasionally they have a spat. So what was the dynamic between Drew and Debi? "We get along really well," says Barrymore. "We're easygoing, we laugh a lot, and it's not fake. We really do genuinely like each other, which is nice."

debi

Spice mazar

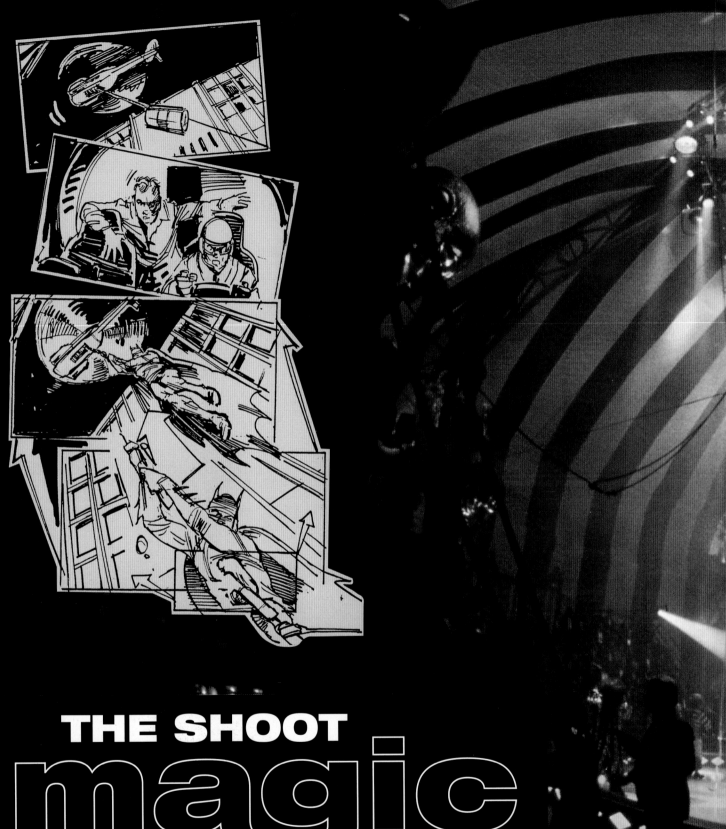

THE SHOOT
magic
on a daily
basis

the production team

peter macgregor-scott

PRODUCER

It has been suggested that if some enterprising film-maker ever decided to launch a remake of the classic adventure films *Gunga Din* or *The Lives of a Bengal Lancer*, he would do well to bring Peter Macgregor-Scott on as producer. Not only would the British-born Scott manage to orchestrate the activities of a cast and crew of thousands, but he could probably double his services by getting into period khakis and portraying a classic Sergeant-Major in Her Majesty's army! With his noble moustache, English accent and most of all, abilities to marshal logistically difficult productions from the earliest stages of pre-production through and beyond release, Macgregor-Scott embodies a proud tradition which he puts into the service of fighting a different kind of war ... moviemaking.

There are basically two kinds of producers in Hollywood: those who actually do the job, and those who don't. Macgregor-Scott is one of the stalwarts in the first grouping, known and respected for his expertise in every area of the filmmaking process. Need to find a real, working battleship that could serve as a shooting (literally) location for a few months? Get Macgregor-Scott, who secured the U.S.S. Alabama for the Steven Seagal smash *Under Siege*. Need to mount a spectacular smash-up between a full-sized, multi-car train and a bus? Get Macgregor-Scott, who coordinated this unbelievable feat for yet another big action blockbuster, *The Fugitive*. It was only natural that Warner Bros., the studio responsible for those two films, would once again call upon Macgregor-Scott for their most ambitious production of 1995.

The producer was prepared for what would be expected of him for *Batman Forever*: "The dynamics of this picture are such that to keep the support mechanism fully charged and maintained is quite a full-time operation. I have to be involved in the day-to-day operation of this film; and my major responsibility, I think, is to have vision about what is most practical and economical, and have foresight about where the problems lie. There will always be problems on any production, but as long as you have the solutions, the problems don't really exist."

It might seem that Macgregor-Scott has celluloid running in his veins. His grandfather owned the Rialto Theatre in Maidenhead, England, and his father switched from his original career as a rubber planter to become a cinema salesman and later, a leading British distributor.

Macgregor-Scott moved to the United States from England in 1970, and he worked on his first movie – the Philippines-shot *Ride the Tiger* – that same year.

Working his way up through the ranks of the industry, Macgregor-Scott soon became known as one of the best creative and hands-on producers in the business with such hit comedies as *Cheech & Chong's Next Movie*, *Cheech & Chong Still Smokin'* and *Revenge of the Nerds*. He also produced three films starring Steven Seagal, *Marked for Death*, *Out for Justice* and the aforementioned *Under Siege*. In 1994, Macgregor-Scott returned to his native England to produce Warner Bros.' new version of the family classic *Black Beauty*.

Ever-present on the set and often working into the wee hours, Macgregor-Scott coordinates every minute detail of more than 40 individual departments and two shooting units. How did producing *Batman Forever* compare with his previous films?

Smiles Macgregor-Scott from beneath his moustache: "It's like making three *The Fugitive*s at the same time in different cities!"

tim burton PRODUCER

Tim Burton, the visionary artist who created the highly imaginative and detailed worlds of *Pee-wee's Big Adventure*, *Beetlejuice*, *Batman*, *Edward Scissorhands*, *Batman Returns*, *Tim Burton's The Nightmare Before Christmas* and *Ed Wood*, now returns to Gotham City as a producer of *Batman Forever*.

Burton grew up in Burbank, California, where he sated his imagination's ravenous hunger by watching old horror films and drawing cartoons. His talent was formally recognized in the ninth grade by local trash collectors when he won a prize for an anti-litter poster he designed. His artwork adorned Burbank garbage trucks for a year.

Although Burton has stated that his primary ambition during his formative years was to become the actor who played Godzilla, he settled for being an animator. He attended the Cal Arts Institute on a Disney fellowship and soon after joined Walt Disney Studios as an animator. It was during these early years at Disney that Burton came

up with the idea for *Tim Burton's The Nightmare Before Christmas*, but the studio shelved the project for 10 years until after the success of Batman.

Burton gained experience early at Disney, working on such projects as *The Fox and the Hound* and *The Black Cauldron*, and making his directorial debut with the animated short *Vincent*, an homage to one of Burton's childhood heroes, actor Vincent Price. Narrated by Price himself, the film was a critical success and won a number of awards, including two from the Chicago Film Festival.

Burton's next project for Disney was *Frankenweenie* His first foray into live-action, this inventive twist on Frankenstein told the story of a young boy who brings his dead dog back to life.

In 1985 Burton directed his first feature film, *Pee-wee's Big Adventure*, bringing Paul Reuben's cartoonesque creation, Pee-wee Herman, to vivid life. The same visual power blossomed further in *Beetlejuice* (1988), a supernatural comedy about an amoral ghoul haunting a New England family starring Michael Keaton, Geena Davis, Alec Baldwin and Winona Ryder. An enormous success at the box office, *Beetlejuice* also won the Academy Award for Best Makeup.

In 1989 Burton directed *Batman*, starring Jack Nicholson, Michael Keaton and Kim Basinger. A massive success, the National Association of Theatre Owners (NATO) awarded him the Director of the Year Award for his accomplishment.

Burton next directed and produced *Edward Scissorhands*, starring Johnny Depp, Winona Ryder and Dianne Wiest. One of the biggest hits of the 1990 Christmas season, the film was acclaimed for its wild vision and fairy-tale sensibility. In 1992 Burton once again explored the dark underworld of Gotham City in *Batman Returns*, the highest grossing film that year. *Tim Burton's The Nightmare Before Christmas*, directed by Henry Selick, received extraordinary reviews for its inventiveness and was a major success in the fall of 1993.

In 1994, Burton directed and co-produced *Ed Wood*, starring Johnny Depp as Edward Wood, Jr., the infamous 1950s cross-dressing, cult movie director of films like *Glen or Glenda* and *Plan Nine From Outer Space*. The film won high praise for its re-invention of Wood's amazing life, and won co-star Martin Landau a Golden Globe Award for his portrayal of fading horror star Bela Lugosi.

Burton has also been working on *Conversations With Vincent*, a documentary about the life and career of Vincent Price.

benjamin melniker
& michael uslan
EXECUTIVE PRODUCERS

The New York-based team of Benjamin Melniker and Michael Uslan serve as executive producers on *Batman Forever*, as they did on both *Batman* and *Batman Returns*. They were also producers of the animated feature film *Batman: Mask of the Phantasm* for Warner Bros., as well as the successful live-action motion picture *Swamp Thing* – based on the popular DC Comics character – and its sequel, *The Return of Swamp Thing*.

On the small screen, Melniker and Uslan executive produced the acclaimed PBS mini-series *Three Sovereigns for Sarah* and executive produced CBS' movie-of-the-week, *Robin Cook's 'Harmful Intent'*, based on Cook's best-selling novel.

Melniker and Uslan have been major names in animated television, executive producing the Emmy Award-nominated *Where on Earth is Carmen Sandiego?* (Fox Network), *Fish Police* (CBS), *Swamp Thing* (Fox and USA Networks) and *Dinosaucers* (The Family Channel and USA Network).

Before he became partners with Michael Uslan, Ben Melniker served with MGM for 30 years in various capacities, leading to his position as Executive Vice President of

Below: Executive producers Benjamin Melniker (on the left) and Michael Uslan return to Batman for the third time.

the company and a member of its board of directors. After leaving the studio, he executive-produced the feature films *Mitchell* and *Shoot*.

Michael Uslan is an authority on comic book history, and taught the first accredited college course on comics, at Indiana University in 1971. He is the author of the first textbook on comics, *The Comic Book in America*, in addition to five other books on the subject.

From 1976 to 1980, Uslan served as motion picture production attorney for United Artists. He has authored several other books in addition to his comic book histories, including *Dick Clark's The First 25 Years of Rock and Roll*. Uslan also scripted stories for DC Comics' *Batman* and *The Shadow* and currently writes the internationally syndicated newspaper comic strip *Terry and the Pirates*.

akiva goldsman
SCREENWRITER

Search Hollywood today, and you will find few paths more interesting than that taken by Akiva Goldsman. Born in Brooklyn Heights, New York, and raised in New York City, he is the son of two prominent child psychologists who work with autistic children and who founded the Blueberry Treatment Centers. Goldsman graduated from Wesleyan University and earned his graduate degree in creative writing from New York University. But he began his career by following his parents into the field of mental health.

This unique ability to understand the complex workings of the human mind – combined with a lifelong passion for comic books, particularly the tales of the Dark Knight – made Goldsman the perfect writer to incisively re-invent the legends of Gotham City for *Batman Forever*.

"Working in mental health was great preparation for writing the film," explains Goldsman. "This is a story about duality, and one of the protagonists – Dr. Chase Meridian – is actually a psychiatrist. I think that if one works with other human beings, it inexorably creeps into the soul. And what's remarkable about comic books is that they provide a heightened reality which necessarily must live on a heightened psychological reality."

Goldsman – while providing all of the requisite action for a Batman movie – also chose to carefully sculpt the English language into finely tuned dialogue for the characters. Goldsman's dialogue ranges from the witty, verbal *pas de deux* between the Riddler and Two-Face to the emotional encounters of Bruce Wayne and Chase Meridian.

It is such attention to his craft that has kept Akiva Goldsman much in demand since selling *Silent Fall*, his first script, which was filmed by Bruce Beresford for Morgan Creek and distributed by Warner Bros. in 1994. He first collaborated with Joel Schumacher as the co-writer of the Summer 1994 hit *The Client*, acclaimed by critics and audiences as the best screen adaptation of a John Grisham novel. He also contributed to the screenplay of another Warner success in '94, *The Specialist*.

Goldsman's work didn't end after turning in the screenplay. Instead, he was invited onto the set by Joel Schumacher to put his restlessly creative mind to work on a daily basis, altering and improving the script to suit the organic nature of filmmaking. *Batman Forever* was not only "developed" in the writing process, but during the actual filmmaking as well.

"Joel is nearly unique in the movie business," notes Goldsman, "in that he is utterly collaborative. He feels that, just as the cinematographer, production designer or costume designer are useful in an ongoing fashion by providing input, the writer who helped form the story should be part of the process of making the movie. Any writer would be lucky to be in this situation."

Above: Screenwriter Akiva Goldsman.

Music and Theatre at the University of California at San Diego, he met Janet – a Hollywood native studying linguistics at UCLA – in 1981, and married her two years later. Frustrated that Los Angeles was not a theatre town, but reluctant to move to New York, Lee was urged by Janet to try another medium – film. Lee then encouraged Janet to join him as part of the new endeavor.

The Batchlers wrote the fourth season premiere of the popular CBS series *The Equalizer*, followed by other episodic work and children's videos "to pay the rent." They finally decided that what they really wanted to do was to write feature films, which resulted in their very first effort, *Smoke and Mirrors*, now awaiting production.

The Batchlers have two more projects in active development with major Hollywood studios: *Stanley and Livingstone* at Hollywood Pictures and *Captain Nemo* at Amblin through Universal. They make their home in Brentwood, California with young son Corin and a cat named Mr. Underfoot.

lee batchler & janet scott batchler

SCREENWRITERS

"It's everything we envisioned ... and more," said Lee Batchler and Janet Scott Batchler on one of their visits to the *Batman Forever* set. The Batchlers, partners in both an acclaimed screenwriting affiliation and life itself, made their considerable contributions to *Batman Forever* following the one million dollar sale of their heralded script *Smoke and Mirrors*. It was a quantum career leap for the couple, who had only recently decided to give up episodic television writing for a crack at feature films.

Lee Batchler was born in Farmington, New Mexico and grew up in La Jolla, California. A double major in

stephen goldblatt

DIRECTOR OF PHOTOGRAPHY

If you want to know why the estimable services of Stephen Goldblatt were called upon to serve the massive requirements of *Batman Forever*, you might ask producer Peter Macgregor-Scott.

"What Stephen brought to the film," says Macgregor-Scott, "is absolute abandon to lighting. You have to see it to understand it. It feels like you're living in Batman's world. Gotham has a fantastic look in the movie. His approach and risk-taking are absolutely magnificent. One of the stars of *Batman Forever* is actually Stephen Goldblatt."

Characteristically, the low-key Stephen Goldblatt is a good deal more reticent to bang his own drum. Ever-polite on the set – and absolutely concentrated on getting his day's (or night's) work done – Goldblatt would much rather let his pictures speak for him. If a picture is worth a

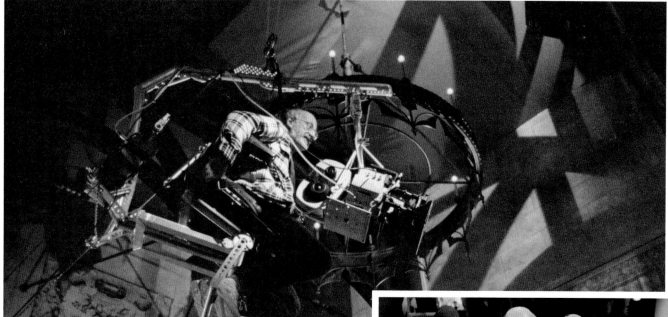

Above: Cinematographer Stephen Goldblatt perched behind the camera high up in the rafters of Wayne Manor on a special rig. *Right:* Cinematographer Stephen Goldblatt (standing) listens as "A" camera operator Ray de la Motte animatedly describes a shot at the Nygmatech party.

thousand words, then ten million of them pour from the screen in *Batman Forever*. Innovation at every turn was Goldblatt's modus operandi, with the hopes that no image or scene would appear connected to what we perceive as everyday life.

"When I was a kid I had a great comic book collection," recalls Goldblatt. "I left South Africa when I was seven, and I remember having to leave my collection behind. So something must have rubbed off. Joel Schumacher and I agreed that we wanted to make everything we could possibly manage in the film, without exception, comic book. So there's almost nothing that I can think of in this film that's of a really ordinary nature."

Batman Forever is photographed in bold, outstanding hues that reflect similarly adventurous coloration in the original Batman comic books. "Also, we set color themes for characters," says Goldblatt. "Batman's are blues and purples and whites. Two-Face is red and magenta. The Riddler is green. Chase is pink. It really bangs out, and that's great about them. We're not trying to be subtle. I really liked it when Joel said from the beginning that he wanted the film to be operatic."

Goldblatt has enjoyed a remarkably fruitful career as a feature film cinematographer after getting his start as a still photographer and then working on a variety of documentaries in England, where his family moved after leaving their native South Africa. His first feature was the 1980 punk drama *Breaking Glass*, followed by Peter Hyams' elaborate science fiction adventure, *Outland*;

Tony Scott's romantic vampire thriller, *The Hunger*; and then Francis Ford Coppola's elaborate period drama, *The Cotton Club*.

Goldblatt has served as director of photography on such films as Barry Levinson's *Young Sherlock Holmes*, Taylor Hackford's *Everybody's All-American*, the Richard Donner hits *Lethal Weapon* and *Lethal Weapon 2*, John Patrick Shanley's *Joe Versus the Volcano*, Alan J. Pakula's *Consenting Adults* and *The Pelican Brief*, Mark Rydell's *For The Boys* and Barbra Streisand's *The Prince of Tides*, which earned him an Academy Award nomination.

Having worked with so many prominent directors, Goldblatt was particularly pleased by his collaboration with Joel Schumacher. "It's been close," notes Goldblatt, "and we've been so in sync about what's right and what looks great. And Joel has been so encouraging, in terms of a fun point of view.

"We've gone for extreme contrast, rich color, moving lights, changes of angle, very unconventional framing and a real, real desire to be true to a genre. I may never get an opportunity to have this kind of freedom again, so I wasn't about to turn down the opportunities that were presented."

On set, Goldblatt's dry British style was often a hilarious contrast to Schumacher's unabashed New York enthusiasm. Following the completion of the elaborate first shot in the Batcave – an extraordinary moment in which one long, fluid camera movement captures the entire mythos of the Dark Knight and his world – the modest Goldblatt articulated a quiet "Very good" in his very British accent.

To which Schumacher responded with a loud "THAT WAS GREAT!!!" Then, turning to his colleague from the other side of the ocean, the director added, "That's American for 'very good,' Stephen."

dennis virkler FILM EDITOR

On movie sets, film editors are often heard of but little seen. Generally, they're locked away in their cutting rooms, wending their way through a thousand miles of film in search of a movie.

But thanks to Joel Schumacher, when *Batman Forever* began principal photography in New York, Dennis Virkler was right there on set, all night, overseeing the integration of production and post-production from the very start.

"Much of film editing is intuition," says Virkler. "You get a feel for what the movie will become in the beginning,

and having been included in four months of pre-production was a tremendous asset."

Dennis Virkler, an Academy Award-nominee for two pulse-pounding action films – John McTiernan's *The Hunt for Red October* and Andrew Davis' *The Fugitive* – is one of the industry's most sought-after editors. Despite his previous work on high-powered, big-budget motion pictures, Virkler faced an even more massive task on *Batman Forever*. It was up to Virkler to assemble footage shot by the first unit, a large second unit and John Dykstra's huge visual effects division, and then come up with a finished product ready for theatres around the world with only three months between the end of principal photography in early March and release in mid-June.

"When you're up against a schedule like that," says Virkler, "one learns to appreciate the high level of communication that exists between all the various departments, because there just isn't enough time to do anything twice."

Following a period of apprenticeships in sound effects and music editing, Virkler finally settled into motion picture editing and served as full editor for the first time on the 1976 horror film *Burnt Offerings*. His credits since then – in addition to *The Hunt for Red October* and *The Fugitive* – have included *Continental Divide*, *Gorky Park*, *Independence Day*, *Distant Thunder*, *Falling From Grace* and *Under Siege*.

elliot goldenthal COMPOSER

"Elliot Goldenthal can do everything," says Joel Schumacher of the composer he chose to create new music for a new Batman. "He can write great film scores, symphonies, operas, musicals. In short, Elliot is the real thing!" The year 1994 truly marked Goldenthal's coming-of-age as a film music composer, earning an Academy Award nomination for his score of *Interview With The Vampire*, and also writing the music for *Cobb*, which starred Tommy Lee Jones.

The New York City-based Goldenthal has credentials that mark him as a most unusual talent. He composed the music and co-wrote the libretto for *Juan Darien – A Carnival Mass*, a theatrical oratorio utilizing people and puppets that is based on the Requiem Mass and was inspired by the short story of the same name by Uruguayan author Horacio Quiroga. *Juan Darien* won Obie Awards for both Goldenthal and the director, Julie Taymor, who is also Goldenthal's wife. The piece garnered the American Arts and Letters Richard Rodgers

Award and the Critics Choice Award at the 1990 Edinburgh Festival.

That same year, Goldenthal was commissioned by ASCAP to compose an orchestral work in celebration of Leonard Bernstein's 70th birthday. The piece, *Shadow Play Scherzo*, was performed by the Brooklyn Philharmonic Orchestra at Town Hall in New York City. Later that year, he was commissioned to compose a new work for the Haydn-Mozart Chamber Orchestra commemorating the 75th anniversary of Ebbets Field, the late, great home of the Brooklyn Dodgers. Melding his love of baseball with his music, Goldenthal created *Pastime Variations: An Ebbets Field Memorial*, which was performed at the Brooklyn Academy of Music.

Goldenthal's other stage credits include a musical based on Thomas Mann's fable, *The Transposed Heads*, performed at Lincoln Center and winner of the first American Music Theatre Festival's Stephen Sondheim Award; *The King Stag*; and the musical *Liberty's Taken*, produced with the collaboration of Ed Sherin and Norman Lear. Goldenthal also composed complete scores for three Shakespearean plays produced at Joseph Papp's Public Theatre in New York.

A native of Brooklyn, Goldenthal studied with Aaron Copland as a youngster and then received his formal musical education at the Manhattan School of Music, where John Corigliano was his mentor. He earned both a BA and a Master's Degree in musical composition.

Goldenthal has written extensively for full orchestra as well as chamber and vocal combinations. Among other awards, he was the first recipient of the Arturo Toscanini Award for Musical Excellence, the New Music for Young Ensembles composition prize and a New York Foundation for the Arts fellowship.

Most recently, Goldenthal composed a remarkably ambitious symphonic/choral work to honor the 20th anniversary of the formal end of the Vietnam War. The work, commissioned by the Pacific Symphony Orchestra, premiered in April 1995 at the Orange County Performing Arts Center in Southern California.

Goldenthal also composes movie music – and greatly praised movie music at that. He wrote the scores for Gus Van Sant's *Drugstore Cowboy*, *Alien 3*, *Fool's Fire* (directed by Julie Taymor for American Playhouse), *Golden Gate* and *Demolition Man* in addition to the more recent *Interview With The Vampire* and *Cobb*.

A frequent visitor to the *Batman Forever* set in both New York and Los Angeles, Goldenthal began absorbing the unique atmosphere of Joel Schumacher's interpreta-

Above: Composer Elliot Goldenthal

tion of the Gotham mythology from the earliest days of production. The 40-year-old composer was well aware that Danny Elfman's music from Tim Burton's two previous Batman films had its own popularity, but Goldenthal was determined to find his own route. "I think that the Elfman and Burton collaboration was incredible," says Goldenthal. "The challenge for me is not to think about that legacy. The movie that Joel Schumacher is making is another issue of the comic book!"

Despite his high honors in the world of "serious" music, Goldenthal reserves an equally high place for film composition. "I think that film music in this country has been maligned," notes the composer. "It's an art form that's quite unique and singular."

Goldenthal lives in New York City with his wife. The two are working on a collaboration of a new opera based on John Gardner's 1971 novel, *Grendel*, which is the Beowulf legend told from the monster's point of view.

the strange and the beautiful

"For some reason, this feels like a bigger job than *Batman Returns*," says key makeup artist Ve Neill, who is more than familiar with "big jobs." With *Batman Forever*, Neill and her colleague, key hair stylist Yolanda Toussieng, stretched the limits of their creativity, which is no small thing. Neill and Toussieng both won Academy Awards for their work on *Mrs. Doubtfire*, in which they transformed Robin Williams into a believable, elderly Scottish nanny. Neill also won an Oscar for Tim Burton's *Beetlejuice* and was nominated for both *Edward Scissorhands* and *Hoffa*. (Toussieng was also nominated for the latter.) All three heads of the Batman Forever makeup and hair team – Ve Neill, Yolanda Toussieng and Rick Baker – each won 1994 Academy Awards for their work together on Tim Burton's *Ed Wood*.

Two of the film's protagonists demanded elaborate and time-consuming makeup on a daily basis: Two-Face and the Riddler.

two-face

The basic makeup scheme for Tommy Lee Jones' Two-Face was designed by yet another dual Oscar winner, the famed special effects and makeup artist Rick Baker (*An American Werewolf in London*, *Harry and the Hendersons*).

Ve Neill explains the complex process of converting Tommy Lee Jones into an intimidating arch-villain. "We haven't altered Rick's great basic concept, just the intricacies of painting his appliances to make them look better on film. The appliances are made of foam latex. For Two-Face, we have a skull piece, a lower lip, an upper lip, a large cheek piece which goes all the way into the corner of an eye and wraps around to the outside of Tommy Lee's temple and onto the headpiece we've also created, which covers one of Tommy Lee's ears. The final piece that we put on is for the forehead.

"The first time we applied Two-Face's makeup to Tommy Lee, it took almost four hours, because we were still experimenting. We eventually refined the process to an hour and forty minutes for makeup and hair. All of the latex appliances are pre-painted, which helps us to make it as expedient as possible."

the riddler

"Jim Carrey actually has four different looks in the film," explains Ve Neill. "He starts out as Edward Nygma, kind of your quintessential science nerd, with horn-rimmed glasses and stringy, shoulder-length auburn hair. He then segues, still as Nygma, into something of a debonair copy of Bruce Wayne. Then there are two looks for the Riddler, one early in the story and another later on after he's expanded his brain on his Box invention."

One of *Batman Forever*'s innovations is the color and style of the Riddler's hair, which is more stylized – even post-"punk" – than the more "normal" manifestations seen in the comics and '60s TV series. "Coming up with that coral hair decision was not easy," says Yolanda Toussieng. "We actually had three wigs made before our first test for the Riddler. One was black, one was white and the other was coral. As soon as Joel Schumacher saw them, he immediately decided on the coral, which he thought was visually appealing and a lot of fun."

Opposite: Fantastic day-glo makeup of a Gotham street gang, influenced by tribal face painting. *Left*: Two-Face's and the Riddler's makeup and hair designs provided big challenges for the Oscar-winning team of Ve Neill (*above left*) and Yolanda Toussieng.

**stunning
stunts**

One of the industry's best of the best at what he does, *Batman Forever* stunt coordinator Conrad Palmisano leads his troops like a tough-but-lovable football coach or a military commander popular with his troops.

He also knows how to create a great action scene, a skill he has had ample opportunity to demonstrate on *Batman Forever*. "Once you start this roller coaster ride you want to keep it going," says Palmisano. "There are highs and lows on the coaster, but you want it to be a terrific ride all the way."

Among other things, Joel Schumacher and Connie Palmisano re-conceptualized the way Batman fights *mano-a-mano*. "He's a lot more mobile and it's a lot more fun," notes Palmisano. "The action will be much faster, much more overlapping, and Batman will seldom be fighting only one guy. Rather, he'll be fighting several at once in a combination of martial arts techniques that I call Gotham Style."

Although more than 100 stunt players were employed by Palmisano for *Batman Forever*, three in particular stood out: Keith Campbell, Alex Daniels and Mitch Gaylord, who was the first American gymnast to ever score a perfect "10" in Olympic history.

While Val Kilmer, Tommy Lee Jones and Chris O'Donnell insisted on performing as many of their own stunts as feasible, sometimes circumstances, common sense and insurance policies prevent stars from putting themselves in mortal danger. That's when the stunt players are called in to do what they do best, which is to risk life and limb on a daily basis.

Campbell, Daniels and Gaylord each had their favorite moment of glory during the course of the *Batman*

Opposite: Stuntman Keith Campbell executes a fabulous somersault at the Nygmatech party. *Below:* Dick Grayson faces off with a menacing gang leader – played by famed kick boxing champion Don "The Dragon" Wilson. *Above:* Multi-medal winning Olympic gymnast Mitch Gaylord performs a daredevil stunt as Dick Grayson high up in the rafters of Wayne Manor.

Forever shoot. For Boise, Idaho native Campbell, a former professional gymnast, it was the Nygmatech party scene climax when Batman plunges through a glass ceiling, drops 40 feet, does an astonishing somersault off a fountain and lands directly on top of two of Two-Face's thugs.

The multi-talented Alex Daniels enjoyed having a few thousand pounds of wood, concrete and dirt fall on him in the scene where the abandoned Gotham Plaza subway station collapses on top of a helpless Batman. "You have to prepare for anything to happen," says Daniels. "I mean, I have a plate in my leg from one that I *didn't* expect a few years ago!"

For Mitch Gaylord – the most decorated Olympic gymnast in American history, winning one gold, one silver and two bronze medals in 1984 – one of his greatest rushes was a remarkable stunt in which he doubled for Chris O'Donnell as Dick Grayson. At a height of more than 40 feet, Gaylord leaped from a Wayne Manor balcony to a beam, from the beam onto a chandelier, then to another beam, climaxing in a stupendous back flip flyaway to the wall, where he grabbed onto a rope hanging from a medieval tapestry, and then dropped, catlike, to the staircase underneath.

"I've never done anything like *that* in gymnastics competition!," Gaylord noted afterwards, to the wild applause of the entire cast and crew.

STRONGHOLD

What a blank canvas is to a painter, an empty soundstage is to a production designer ... a clean slate, waiting to be filled with the contents of the artist's imagination. When a motion picture is set in the "real" world, the production designer must work within the bounds of those parameters. But when the backdrop is wholly imaginary ... the possibilities are endless.

The glorious, intimidating task of creating an all-new, freshly-conceived Gotham City fell to Barbara Ling, who had previously collaborated with Joel Schumacher on *Falling Down* and also designed the sets for such features as *Less Than Zero*, David Byrne's *True Stories*, *Men Don't Leave*, *Fried Green Tomatoes*, *With Honors* and Oliver Stone's *The Doors*.

As the production designer, Ling would not only be responsible for the creation of all sets, but also the vehicles, gadgets, arsenals and other accoutrements utilized by Batman, Robin, Two-Face, the Riddler, Dr. Chase Meridian and the other inhabitants of Gotham. No one could be happier than Ling to receive such a mighty artistic summons.

Barbara Ling grew up in Brentwood, California, and gained degrees in political science and architecture at UCLA. Ling began her career in the theatre, designing sets and lighting for nearly 200 productions, including *Women Behind Bars* in Los Angeles and San Francisco, and *Beyond Therapy* at the Los Angeles Public Theatre. In addition to her film and theatre work, Ling also designed the sets and lighting for numerous concert tours, including David Byrne's world tour in 1990. Her penchant for adventurous theatricality would serve Ling well for her *Batman Forever* work, which consistently transcended conventional expectations.

Barbara Ling created almost 60 sets for *Batman Forever* (nearly 40 more than the previous Batman film), assisted by art directors Chris Burian-Mohr, James Hegedus, Joseph P. Lucky and a talented staff of set designers, illustrators, model makers, a computer graphics artist, secretaries and departmental assistants. While there are respectful nods in the design of the new Gotham City to the marvelous work done by Anton Furst for *Batman* and Bo Welch for *Batman Returns*, Ling and Joel Schumacher decided from day one to eschew any sense of deja vu in their version of the legend. Everything – from the Batcave to the Batmobile – would be completely different. "I'm a very big fan of Anton's and Bo's work," says Ling, "but I think it's exciting to use new people and ideas on everything you do. The Batman comics do not reflect any one thing. What's kept them alive,

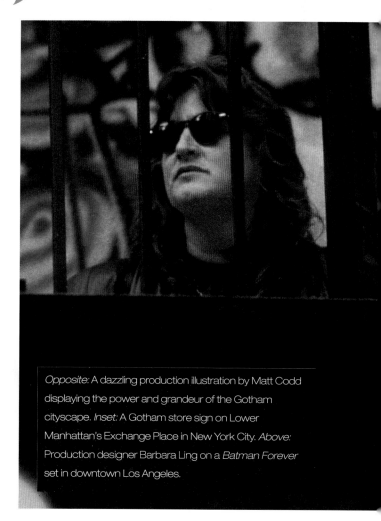

Opposite: A dazzling production illustration by Matt Codd displaying the power and grandeur of the Gotham cityscape. *Inset:* A Gotham store sign on Lower Manhattan's Exchange Place in New York City. *Above:* Production designer Barbara Ling on a *Batman Forever* set in downtown Los Angeles.

I think, is that with each illustrator and each new art director, it all changes. It's always exciting and different."

"I thought that part of the fun of doing Gotham would be to create our own city," adds Schumacher. "Bob Kane more or less based Gotham on New York, so we're using parts of Manhattan and parts of Los Angeles, and making up the rest."

gotham city
the concept

"When I first approached the design of Gotham," says Ling, "my mind always went to the World's Fair idea of buildings and statues being so overscaled that man is stunted. Gotham City is designed to be three times the height of New York, with everything on a monumental level. We examined lots of photos and films of the great World's Fairs of the '20s, '30s and '40s, which were filled with tiny people staring in awe at tremendous buildings."

Above: Another fabulous production illustration, by Matt Codd and Mauro Borrelli, of the daunting Gotham cityscape. *Right*: One of the impressive Gotham statues, bathed in blue light.

Ling and Schumacher wanted a Gotham that transcended all times and places, melding elements of Art Deco, Russian Constructivism, European and American futurism, modernism and post-modernism. In *Batman Forever*, Gotham rises to the heavens, its massive edifices traversed by sky-high roadways and bridges. The production designer and the director also decided to avoid a monochromatic vision of Gotham, turning instead to the original comic books for inspiration.

"We were very influenced by the comics," notes Ling, "which, beginning in the 1940s, always had these wonderful color washes in the frames. In one panel, the wash would be red, and in the next scene, blue. That was very striking to us, and we felt that it was an important element to capture. After all, the comics weren't black and white. Instead, they always reflected these strange washes of lights. From the very beginning we knew that it was going to be a pattern and look for the city. It's a great way of looking at Gotham."

Assisting Barbara Ling in conceptualizing Gotham were some of the industry's most talented production illustrators, including Marty Kline, Brent Boats, Joe Griffith, Sean Hargreaves and Oliver Scholl.

Ling also brought production design into the cybertech age by calling upon the creative skills of computer graphics artist Mary Locatell. Together, Ling and Locatell worked out elaborate, multi-layered designs and concepts for Gotham through revolutionary digital compositing. "This way," explains Ling, "we can visualize in a couple of hours what it takes days to produce through more conventional methods."

And since Bob Kane had originally based his concept of Gotham on the city in which he created Batman – New York – why not return to that very city for the initial shoot of *Batman Forever*?

gotham
in the big apple

"I wish we could have done a month of work in New York," says Ling, "but in fact, we only shot there for a week. I picked out a unique street in Lower Manhattan, which gave us the kind of narrowness and height quality of what Gotham is to me, which is towering corridors of buildings looming over tightly packed avenues.

"Exchange Place – just one block from Wall Street itself – has that amazing illusion. Then we added 35 and 40-foot tall sculptures and ended up putting in overscaled signage that helped take what is already the giant molding of New York and make it look even bigger. We had colored steam and smoke pouring out of the sidewalk grilles, which created another sense of scale where it looks like the sidewalks are melting into the ground."

For the exterior of the Ritz Gotham Hotel – where Bruce Wayne, Dick Grayson and Chase Meridian arrive for the Nygmatech party – producer Peter Macgregor-Scott, New York unit production manager Peter Pastorelli and East Coast location manager Christian von Tippelskirsch helped Ling secure the old U.S. Customs Building, just weeks before it reopened as the Smithsonian Museum of the American Indian. Gold lame draping, gold carpets leading up the grand staircase, flickering gold gas lamps and synchronized lighting and moving projections made the exterior look like a conceptual art exhibit.

Says Ling, "To me there is no design on film without light. As I learned in theatre, it doesn't matter how beautiful a set you have if it's not well lit. And moving, three-dimensional light is probably the most under-used thing in film."

For the exterior of Wayne Manor, the company traveled to Long Island, where the Webb Institute of Naval Architecture stood in for Bruce Wayne's imposing home. This exterior is somewhat more modest than those seen in the previous two films.

"Joel and I had gone through many thoughts and ideas about Wayne Manor," explains Ling. "Should we go to England and shoot the same palatial house that was used in the first film? But Joel wanted to keep Bruce Wayne on a more accessible level – for him to have a monumentally proportioned house, but not something that is frightening or takes you away from learning about him.

Main picture: The exterior of Wayne Manor, actually the Webb Institute in Glen Cove, Long Island. *Inset above:* The imposing entrance to the Nygmatech party, filmed at the old U.S. Customs Building in New York's Wall Street district.

wayne enterprises
office complex

"Instead," continues the designer, "we used elements to help throw it off a bit. Gigantic horse sculptures frame the house, which gives Bruce a sense of being a collector of statuary." These sculptures – designed by Ling and executed by head sculptor Yarek Alfer and his crew from polyurethane foam (which looks strikingly like stone when properly painted) – were 22 feet tall, just two of dozens of sculptural pieces that would be required for the film.

To explore the character and nature of Bruce Wayne, three environments were designed by Ling: the Wayne Manor interior, the Batcave and the Wayne Enterprises office complex.

"In making Bruce Wayne's office," says Ling, "we decided he would work in an environmentally correct space in the middle of this relatively decaying, polluted city. The office building is on a hydraulic dam. Bruce uses clean water energy, a contrast to the Riddler's filth-spewing Claw Island complex. The interior has a clean feeling, except for Edward Nygma's chaotic work station, which really sticks out like the proverbial sore thumb. The Wayne Enterprises research laboratory is 150 feet long, with the illusion of being 200 feet. Bruce's office is 30 feet high and 60 feet long and is quite austere and minimalist. Again, it's a contrast to the clutter that surrounds Edward Nygma and Two-Face."

The electronics division of Wayne Enterprises is a delicious

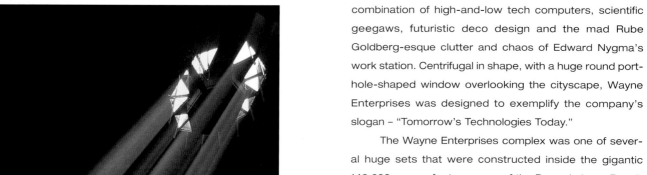

combination of high-and-low tech computers, scientific geegaws, futuristic deco design and the mad Rube Goldberg-esque clutter and chaos of Edward Nygma's work station. Centrifugal in shape, with a huge round porthole-shaped window overlooking the cityscape, Wayne Enterprises was designed to exemplify the company's slogan – "Tomorrow's Technologies Today."

The Wayne Enterprises complex was one of several huge sets that were constructed inside the gigantic 140,000 square foot expanse of the Dome in Long Beach that once housed the Spruce Goose, Howard Hughes' mammoth World War II-era aircraft. Several other important sets were built in the Dome, including one absolutely central to the entire myth of the Dark Knight...

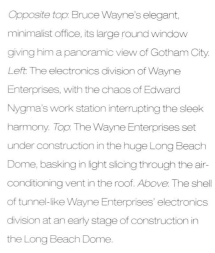

Opposite top: Bruce Wayne's elegant, minimalist office, its large round window giving him a panoramic view of Gotham City. *Left:* The electronics division of Wayne Enterprises, with the chaos of Edward Nygma's work station interrupting the sleek harmony. *Top:* The Wayne Enterprises set under construction in the huge Long Beach Dome, basking in light slicing through the air-conditioning vent in the roof. *Above:* The shell of tunnel-like Wayne Enterprises' electronics division at an early stage of construction in the Long Beach Dome.

the batcave

"I was determined to have a 'real' Batcave this time, and not be talked into doing it as a matte painting with a small set inserted," insists Barbara Ling. "The biggest difference, for me, between this and the other Batcaves was that I wanted to put in elements of

architecture. I wanted audiences to have the feeling that Batman really worked on building this cave – it's not just carved out of rock. We have a 'beehive wall' with Batman's video monitor, armatures holding the cave up, arches that lead into the cave and a gigantic iron vault that holds the Batsuits, weapons and gadgetry."

Rising more than 60 feet above the floor of the Spruce Goose Dome, looming over the cast and crew with its black-blue ridges and mysterious crevices, the Batcave of *Batman Forever* was, appropriately, a world in itself. The world in which Bruce Wayne/Batman, Alfred and eventually Robin keep a watchful eye on Gotham City from deep beneath its surface. Multi-leveled, with work stations for both Bruce and Alfred (featuring electronic and surveillance equipment that fancifully combines 21st

century high technology with materials that might seem more at home in Dr. Frankenstein's laboratory), the Batcave also features a unique carport for the Batmobile. Rising from the depths of the cave, light slicing through its grate as it revolves, its metal walkways (without guard-rails ... very scary) connecting the work stations with the Batmobile turntable. The carport was a most dramatic creation ...

As was the entire Batcave. Let's face it: anybody who has ever seen, read or heard Batman in any of his manifestations has wanted to visit the Batcave. It's not only Batman Central – it's just flat-out cool ... and never so cool as it is in *Batman Forever*.

Ling designed another surprise for Batman fans: the cave *beneath* the cave – the Subterranean Batcave, a heretofore unseen marvel at the base of Gotham's river. In the Subterranean Batcave, Batman keeps hidden two of his extraordinary crime fighting vehicles – the Batboat and, suspended from the cave ceiling like the animal it was designed to resemble, the Batwing!

wayne manor

interior

Also constructed inside the Long Beach Dome, the Wayne Manor interior set is 40 feet high, 150 feet long and 50 feet wide. Three stories high, imposing and just a little gloomy, the interior of Wayne Manor is not unlike William Randolph Hearst's San Simeon (or, for that matter, Charles Foster Kane's Xanadu). There's a feeling of melancholy, loneliness and solitude, particularly in the massive grand foyer, with its huge chandelier and hanging medieval tapestries. The library is warmer in tone, featuring a fireplace that is almost big enough to garage a Bentley and a circular steel staircase leading to fine, antique volumes of literature.

Opposite top: Batman and Alfred's crime lab. *Opposite center*: The Batcave under construction in the Dome, rising more than 60 feet from the floor. *Inset*: The Batcave in its complete majesty, with the Batmobile rising on its lift.

Top: The imposing staircase inside in the Wayne Manor entrance hall. It is adorned with a huge chandelier and medieval tapestries. *Above*: The more human dimensions of the Wayne Manor library, with its elegant but enormous fireplace.

two-face's lair

In contrast to the relative normalcy of Bruce Wayne's existence, Barbara Ling also created environments for the nemeses of Bruce Wayne (and Batman): Two-Face and the Riddler.

"I don't know why, but I always thought that Two-Face should live inside of a bridge," explains Ling. "We scouted every bridge in New York, and finally decided upon the Manhattan Bridge – which has a rather magnificent facade – for the establishing shot. Then the challenge was to create the inside of that lair, which we did in the Spruce Goose Dome.

"We decided to build a stone and steel interior, with a large Gothic element in the arches, which is gnarly and brambled. And then, of course, everything is split right down the middle, representing Two-Face's good side and bad side. So the set is red on his dark side, and kind of light and creamy on his light side. It was a lot of fun to design and build.

the riddler's lair

""I always thought that the Riddler should live in a totally round world," Ling says, "to offset him against the cragginess of Two-Face's Lair and the austerity and linearness of Bruce Wayne's environments. The idea evolved into a kind of decayed refinery that the Riddler eventually restores into his central power station for sucking the brainpower of all Gotham City. So we ended up with an 80-foot round by 50-foot high green ball on Stage 16, the biggest soundstage at Warner Bros. in Burbank."

By any standard, the Riddler's Lair was an amazing creation. A circular pathway leads up iron latticework to the Riddler's grandiose throne, bookended by replicas of

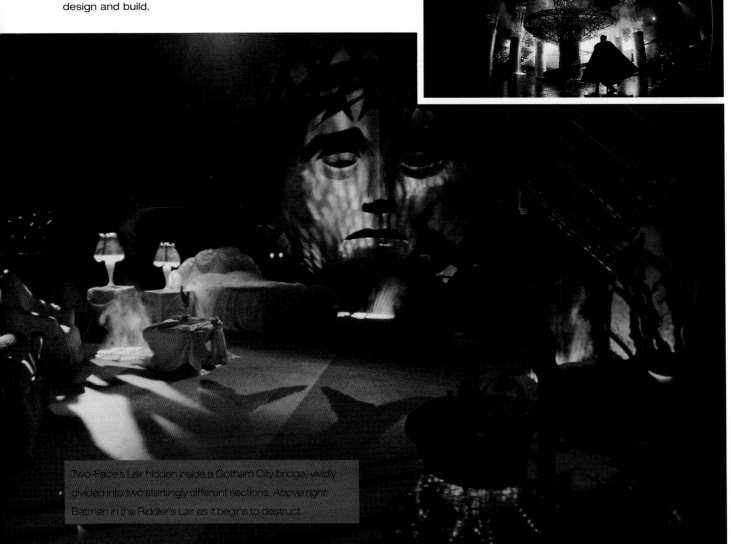

Two-Face's Lair hidden inside a Gotham City bridge, vividly divided into two startlingly different sections. *Above right:* Batman in the Riddler's Lair as it begins to destruct.

Riddler. I wanted Edward Nygma, in the beginning, to be extremely cluttered in his office space and tiny basement apartment. Then he starts to emulate Bruce Wayne in his own demented way, which finally leads to the Riddler's Lair. The Lair is all about power. There's very little else that's important to the Riddler, at that point in the story."

Also constructed – on Universal Studios Stage 12, within shouting distance of Warner Bros.' Burbank studios – was the large cylinder upon which the Riddler's domed Lair rests. Riddled with cut out question marks, through which cinematographer Stephen Goldblatt burned high-intensity lights, this is the locale for the film's stunning showdown between Batman, Robin, Chase Meridian and on the other side of the coin, Two-Face and the Riddler.

Rodin's "Thinker" sculptures. Four gigantic plasma tubes (intentionally resembling old-fashioned television vacuum tubes) surge with cerebral power drained from Gotham's citizenry. On the floor, the Riddler's signature question marks radiate with green light, echoing the green light that pulsates from the entire dome. A bank of computerized lights swivel in any and all directions, creating a stupendous light show when the megalomaniacal Riddler wants to confound his "guests."

Explains Ling, "The main thing is that we watch the growth of this character who comes to be known as the

Above: Barbara Ling and computer graphics artist Mary Locatell converted a photograph of Alcatraz Island with the San Francisco skyline in the background into a conceptual vision of Claw Island with Gotham City in the background.
Below: The remarkable interior of the Riddler's Lair, with the Riddler's throne platform and giant tubes storing the brainpower of the people of Gotham.

68

FOREVER

chase meridian's
office and apartment

There's nothing average-looking in the Gotham City of Joel Schumacher and Barbara Ling, and that includes the office and apartment of criminal psychiatrist Dr. Chase Meridian (Nicole Kidman).

"Everything in Chase's world is caramels and deep lavenders outlined in black," says Ling. "Her office is simple, yet very rich. It was inspired by the interior of one of my favorite New York buildings, the Surrogate Court Building (utilized in *Batman Forever* for the Gotham Police Headquarters). Chase's apartment is actually inspired by a room in the Prague Castle, which I particularly love. It has a very unusual, art nouveau feeling, and I liked putting that feeling around her at home. It's a soft change against the deco and modernistic style of most of the men in the movie."

Chase's apartment, indeed, is almost cathedral-like, with its one large space separated from the much smaller kitchen area by a wall that wittily features a painted fresco in antique style ... as if Michelangelo had snuck into the apartment while Chase was out chasing Batman.

second bank
of gotham vault

This austere space, built on Warner Bros. Stage 16, is the setting for one of the film's most important action sequences, when the Dark Knight interrupts Two-Face and his thugs as they stage their heist of a giant steel safe. The Second Bank of Gotham vault is actually supposed to be 22 stories above the Pan-Asia Town section of Gotham (more on that later).

"The Second Bank of Gotham is in what I call New Gotham," says Ling. "The higher you go in Gotham, the more recent the construction, so that at its

Above: Dr. Chase Meridian's beautiful office, with the Rorshach inkblots in which Bruce Wayne detects the outline of a bat.
Right and inset: Two views of Chase Meridian's unique apartment, which Barbara Ling based on a room in Prague Castle.

upper levels we're more into a modern futurism. My greatest influences in the design of this set are the Japanese futurists, and it's really an ode to Shin Takamatsu of that group. Concrete and steel, very simple geometrics, with only a dollop of color. The safe to me is like a great piece of modernistic sculpture in the center of the room, as if the room were built just for the safe in a ceremonial way."

pan-asia town

"Pan-Asia Town is a collection of styles and architecture, old and new, Asian high-tech versus small, tiny, stacked up streets," explains Ling of this hybrid section of Gotham City. "We actually looked for a long time to find a great element of architecture that would work for the exterior Bank of Gotham, and we found an area on Figueroa Street in Los Angeles that had – ironically – a Japanese-built office building.

"Figueroa Street itself is like a huge freeway," continues Ling. "So we built a small section of Pan-Asia Town, put it on rolling wagons and built a construction site next to the existing building we found … 100 feet of one-story high Pan-Asia storefronts with neon signs. We narrowed a six-lane street into one tiny, narrow lane, and brought out motion lights to liven it all up graphically."

With the later addition of mattes, miniatures and computer-generated imagery from John Dykstra's visual effects department, Pan-Asia Town would take on its full dimensions as envisioned by Ling.

gotham nightlife and alleyway

Ling designed another impressive Gotham exterior to be constructed on Hennessy Street, the Warner Bros. backlot, New York-style street that has been used by hundreds of films since it was built by legendary production designer Dale Hennessy in the late 1930s.

"We're using two streets on the Hennessy set," explains Ling. "The first is the strip through which Dick Grayson drives the Batmobile, which he's taken for a 'spin.' It's sort of a Melrose Avenue, L.A. gone bad, or 8th Avenue in New York City. You know, rotten clubs, old bars, pizza parlors. It's like a section that would have been just off of Times Square. We have glowing colored sculptures lit from behind, animated electric billboards, lots of strange street people."

The back alley is where Dick rescues a young woman from a street gang attired in day-glo costumes and body paint, only to have to face them himself, in one of the film's top martial arts fight sequences. A masterpiece of post-apocalyptic expressionism, the alleyway features "giant graphic elements of graffiti, but all done in ultra-violet paint lit with incandescent lights."

Above: The 100-foot-long rollaway of Pan-Asia Town storefronts. *Right:* The Batmobile speeds through the "Gotham Nightlife" set. *Above right:* Another conceptual computer graphics image designed by Mary Locatell.

police headquarters rooftop

Home to the Bat-Signal, Gotham City's elevated clarion call to the Dark Knight, is the lofty rooftop of the megalopolis' police headquarters. And home to the Gotham Police Headquarters Rooftop set was Warner Stage 15, which coincidentally was also where Bo Welch built his Gotham rooftops set for *Batman Returns*.

The rooftop was inspired by two great Art Deco buildings – 60 Wall Street in New York and the Eastern Building in Los Angeles. Ling also created the monumental sculpted Mayan-style heads as "soldiers" that guard the sacredness of this industrial-strength Bat-Signal, almost as if it's a religious object.

abandoned plaza subway station

Pursuing Two-Face and his gang of thugs after they have blasted their way into the Nygmatech party, Batman leaps off the Ritz Gotham Hotel balcony and into a long tube that dumps him directly into the remains of an abandoned Gotham Plaza subway station. This gorgeous, eerie, atmospheric set was also built on Stage 15 at Warner Bros. (after the Gotham Rooftop set was disassembled).

"Some years ago, working on a different project with Joel Schumacher, we spent weeks in New York trying to look at all of the subway stations not open to the public," explains Ling. "We finally managed to get into the original City Hall station, and it was one of the most stunning train stations I've ever seen. It was opened in the 1920s but within 10 years the trains outgrew it, so the station was closed and almost nobody had seen it since. It's beautiful, with green and cream-colored turn-of-the-century tiles, and stained glass panels on the ceilings.

"The image of this place has always been very strong for me, and it was the inspiration for the abandoned Gotham Plaza subway station that we built. I mixed elements of the Moscow subway with that City Hall station, making it even more Gothic, even Tudor-esque. We scattered broken figurative sculptures about, gigantic portions of a head, a hand, a piece of a foot."

Since the Gotham Plaza station is being torn down rather than restored, Ling and her crew first built the station in pristine condition, and then tore it to shreds. That's deconstructionism, Hollywood-style.

the hippodrome
gotham circus

The last of the mammoth sequences filmed for *Batman Forever*, the Gotham Circus scenes take place inside the Hippodrome, a fabulous throwback to the elephantine arenas of yesteryear. Here we meet Dick Grayson for the first time as a member of The Flying Graysons.

"We'd always thought of the Gotham Circus as being a mixture, like combining Cirque de Soleil and German Expressionism," says Ling. "I liked the idea that there's a tent inside of the Hippodrome, so it's a building within a building. Also, once again, we use figurative sculptures in gigantic proportion, giant men holding up the girders on which the fabric for the tent is mounted. And there are huge Japanese *taiko* drums on top of each platform, with strangely attired drummers banging away. It's not your typical circus!"

Opposite: Batman and Chase rendezvous under the Bat-Signal on the Gotham Police Headquarters rooftop.
Above: The extravagant and colorful Gotham Circus.
Right: The Nygmatech party in full swing.

nygmatech party

When Edward Nygma throws a bash promoting Nygmatech's magical, wondrous "Box," for the upper echelon of Gotham society he does it in style ... Nygma-style, that is. That means enough gold lame fabric to keep every Las Vegas lounge singer happy for a decade, flashing lights, phantasmagoric moving projections, and, as a grand centerpiece, a huge, revolving version of the Box itself sprouting out of a spurting fountain.

The site secured by location manager Laura Sode-Matteson and her associate, Val Kim, was one of Hollywood's landmarks: the Pantages Theatre, situated just by the intersection of Hollywood and Vine. The Pantages is an authentic, living and thriving artifact of Hollywood's Golden Age. Designed by B. Marcus Priteca and constructed in 1929, this movie palace-turned-theatre and concert hall housed the Nygmatech Party in its "zig-zag moderne" lobby, rendered unrecognizable by the visual alterations designed by Ling and her crew.

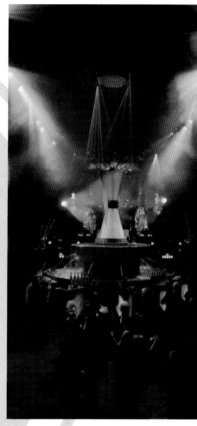

The fountain and revolving Box centerpiece were constructed around the refreshments concession, and the existing statuary was spruced up to conceptually co-exist with their fellow Gothamesque sculptures.

There were still more locations and sets ... the fabulous downtown Los Angeles Theatre, built in 1931 by architect S. Charles Lee, who never would have imagined that its downstairs salon would house Gotham's Excelsior Grand Casino ... the Long Beach Harbor, the site for a terrific action sequence with the sleek Batboat ... Ling's expressionistic set for Arkham Asylum, all medieval forced perspectives and odd angles ... Edward Nygma's bizarre basement apartment, a jumble of electronic equipment, pictorial shrines to Bruce Wayne and a full-sized version of "The Guesser," the mechanical fortune teller that is the physical foundation of Nygma's new persona, the Riddler ... an oil refinery in Carson, California, which would later be converted through the magic of John Dykstra's special effects into the Riddler's Claw Island.

With *Batman Forever*, Barbara Ling ascends into an exclusive top-ranked group of production designers who have set the sky as their limit ... and then pushed beyond it. Gotham City will never be the same.

COSTUME DESIGN
building the better batman

There are basically two reasons why the Dark Knight looks so different in *Batman Forever* than he did in the two previous movies. One, of course, is that he's now played by Val Kilmer. The other is that Bob Ringwood designed his armor-like outfit. Or perhaps we should say that Bob Ringwood *re-designed* the Batsuit again. Although Ringwood worked on all three Batman movies, the Batsuit hasn't been the same in any of the three films.

Left: The Dark Knight. *Above:* Costume designer Bob Ringwood on the Gotham Nightlife set. Above right: Ingrid Ferrin. *Right:* Bruce Wayne works in the Batcave crime lab.

Just as Joel Schumacher wished to update every element of Batman on film, Ringwood was also determined to carry forth everything he and his crew had learned from *Batman* and *Batman Returns*.

As with *Batman Returns*, the enormity of the task created the need for Ringwood to join with a second costume designer, splitting the characters between them. On *Batman Forever*, the British-born Ringwood worked with the Australian-born Ingrid Ferrin, and the two of them developed a visionary alliance.

Generally speaking, Ringwood would design costumes for the colorfully costumed characters (Batman, Robin, Two-Face, the Riddler, Two-Face's thugs, the alley street gang) while Ferrin would concentrate on the less extreme togs donned by Bruce Wayne, Dick Grayson and Dr. Chase Meridian ... plus the somewhat more extreme clothes worn by Sugar and Spice.

Ringwood and Ferrin's backgrounds emphasize quality and accomplishment. Ringwood spent 14 years designing costumes for almost 200 ballet, opera and stage productions in England, Japan, Germany and Holland before winning his first film assignment, George Cukor's television movie, *The Corn Is Green*. He was then hired by John Boorman to create the costumes for the big-budget *Excalibur*, followed by the science fiction epic *Dune* for director David Lynch. Ringwood was asked by Steven Spielberg to design nearly 10,000 costumes for his production of *Empire of the Sun*, and was nominated for an Academy Award for his efforts. Ringwood has also designed the clothing for such diverse motion pictures as *Prick Up Your Ears*, *The Draughtman's Contract*, *Alien[3]*, *Demolition Man*, *The Shadow* and, of course, *Batman* and *Batman Returns*.

Ingrid Ferrin worked with Joel Schumacher as costume designer of *The Client*. In her native country, she was costume designer with the Australian Ballet, and in the U.S. she worked on Broadway and then as wardrobe mistress/costume designer during the first season of the Los Angeles Opera. Segueing into the world of film, Ferrin created the costumes for such features as *Love at Large*, *Golden Gate* and *Born To Be Wild*, in addition to *The Client*.

batman bruce wayne

In *Batman Forever*, the Dark Knight begins the film in his "traditional" suit, and for the finale he dons the new, improved, sonar-equipped "high tech" suit for the first time ever. This meant that Ringwood not only had to design a brand-new suit for Batman, but a revised "traditional" version as well.

The creation, fabrication and implementation of the Batsuit is a rigorous, painstaking process that involves the work of designers, costumers, sculptors, foamers, molders and even a "Batsuit Wrangler" who handles every aspect of

Above: Batman's "traditional" suit, completely redesigned for *Batman Forever. Right:* Stages of preparation for the Batsuit, including detailed clay models and patterns.

these durable but delicate costumes on set. In addition to Bob Ringwood, some of his crew – like Head Batsuit Maker Phil Reynolds, Batsuit Wrangler Day Murch, Model and Mold Designer Ray Tricker and Bat Cape Maker Paul Barrett-Brown – had worked on the first *Batman* in England, and spent much time in America laboring on *Batman Returns* prior to their assignment on *Batman Forever.*

"This time we used all the lessons that we learned on the first two movies," says Ringwood. "The Batsuits are more flexible, lighter, stronger. Joel Schumacher was very keen that he wanted the 'traditional' version of the

Batsuit to be very sleek and sexy, like a panther. By chance, we have a very sleek and sexy actor in Val Kilmer, which helps."

For the traditional suit, Ringwood synthesized the sculpted muscles of the Batsuit from *Batman*, and the more streamlined, abstract version from *Batman Returns.* "We stylized all the muscles, and kept the suit more anatomical," says the designer. "I give a lot of credit to Jose Fernandez, the head sculptor, who made a great contribution to both of Batman's suits, and to Miles Teves, who sculpted Robin's high-tech suit." Ringwood allowed both Fernandez and Teves a great deal of freedom in perfecting the costumes, utilizing pictorial references for inspiration – including photographs of streamlined locomotives and swift, svelte animals.

"For the high-tech suit, I was thinking of things like 1950s chrome grilles on cars," explains Ringwood. "We tried to make it the logical next step of what Batman would wear in a new phase of his crimefighting career."

The high-tech Batsuit is a wonder of fantasy design, at once classical and futuristic, its metallic silver color brilliantly reflecting light. The anatomical detail is further stylized, and the suit features sonar screens that flip down over Batman's eyes in the cowl. There are also small rockets mounted on his boots that give him a terrific thrust to get in (or out) of secret places or dangerous situations.

Just as the exact formula of the Batsuit is a mystery to all in Gotham but Batman and Alfred, the actual "recipe" of materials that make up the costumes is a carefully guarded secret. "It's just like baking a cake," says Batsuit Wrangler Day Murch mischievously. But up to 40 duplicates of both the Batsuit and Robin's high tech suit were created for the production, which means that 120 "cakes" were baked.

Ingrid Ferrin describes the Bruce Wayne costumes as "very wealthy, very sophisticated. Joel wanted Bruce in dark colors. He wanted him to be very mysterious. We repeatedly see the black turtleneck, black cashmere blazer, cocoa brown pants, dark brown suede shoes, charcoal grey pinstriped suits. It's just all very clean and very rich in color."

two-face

Ringwood really unleashed his wilder impulses on the several different costumes he designed for Tommy Lee Jones' Two-Face. Literally reflecting the character himself, the costumes are split exactly down the middle, from collar to footwear, between the conservative district attorney that he once was, and the maniacal fiend that he has become. The color scheme of Two-Face's makeup is also maintained in his clothing. "Of course, Two-Face's 'bad' side is much more fun to do than the 'good' side," says Ringwood. "But we've tried not to slip into camp or kitsch, because if you slip over that edge, you no longer support the actor.

"My feeling is that Tommy Lee has to still have somewhere to go beyond the costume," continues Bob Ringwood, "and that's the same with Batman and everybody else. You can't overpower the actor with the costume. Instead, you want to go to the very edge of the cliff ... and let the actor push it over!"

the riddler
edward nygma

Coming up with the myriad designs for Edward Nygma and his alter-ego, the Riddler, presented Ringwood with one of his greatest but most enjoyable challenges. Nygma undergoes a metamorphosis into the Riddler, and then the Riddler himself advances stage-by-stage into

Above left: Costume sketch by Carlos Huente of one of Two-Face's outfits. *Above right:* The Riddler in his more eccentric stage. *Above:* Two-Face in full bifurcated glory. *Right:* Ed Nygma.

dr. chase | meridian

"Chase is a woman in a man's world," says Ingrid Ferrin, "so when she's in her business attire, she wears elegant suits. But when she goes into a seductive mode in her pursuit of Batman – as she does on the rooftop of the Gotham Police Headquarters – she's just flat-out, drop-dead gorgeous in a black satin, low-cut slip dress. And Nicole Kidman has just the kind of beauty to bring those contrasts out beautifully."

Although Chase doesn't don a costume to hide her identity from the world, as do Batman, Robin, Two-Face and the Riddler, she also has something of a dual personality.

"Again, Joel asked me to go with a particular color palette," continues Ferrin. "Because of that, and the fact that Nicole is so uniquely stunning and tall, we built most of her clothes from the bottom up rather than off the rack, choosing our own fabrics and styles."

increased megalomania and extravagance. "There are many looks, but they all are very identifiable as the Riddler," says Ringwood. "We've never gone outside the fact that he's a man dressed in question marks. We tried to play with it a good deal. We went from the traditional green body suit and jacket with bowler hat familiar from the comic book to a '60s-style 'Nehru Jacket' to what I call the Liberace version and the bizarre electric suit.

"That's because his character gets more and more insane," explains the designer. "He starts out as a shy, timid, unfashionably dressed little computer nerd, and then becomes a rich, successful, grotesque extrovert. So we just echoed that with the clothes. And with Jim Carrey, you can't get too extreme. That man could wear anything. He's great fun to work with."

Top left: The Riddler in one of his more garish suits. *Left:* An original sketch by Carlos Huente of a Riddler costume concept. *Above right:* Chase Meridian escorted in style to the Nygmatech party. *Right:* Chase Meridian in full seductive mode.

robin | dick grayson

Everyone familiar with the story of Batman knows that Robin is attired in a bright green, yellow and red suit (originally patterned by Bob Kane on Errol Flynn's costume in *The Adventures of Robin Hood*), and *Batman Forever* pays homage to this tradition. But just as Bob Ringwood re-invented Batman's look in the 1989 film, so he brings Chris O'Donnell's Robin into the '90s with a new incarnation: a high-tech suit that's a brilliant match for the updated sonar suit worn by Batman in the final scenes of the movie.

"Robin is, in a way, a young, embryonic version of Batman," says Ringwood. "That's what we've done with the costume ... make his suit a companion to Batman's. We carried through the basic style and colors of the traditional Robin costume and tried to echo them in an advanced way. Rather than vibrant primary versions of green, red and yellow, they're now sort of a subdued dark metallic green and dark metallic magenta."

Ingrid Ferrin created the costumes for Dick Grayson, and dressed him "like what he is, which is a circus gypsy. We created some fabulous T-shirts with Russian circus graphics, and he wears an old '50s Chicago police leather jacket with old medals and stickpins, as if he's traveled around the world collecting these things. For accessories, Dick has a Tibetan bracelet on his wrist and another little Indian bracelet, as well as a small string of red beads around his neck. We also created a wonderful belt with an abstract dragon buckle."

Top and top right: Two Carlos Huente concept sketches of Robin's traditional suit and "high-tech" outfit. Costumes and Robin hair styles were both altered for the actual filming. *Above:* Chris O'Donnell in Robin's final "high-tech" suit. *Right:* Bruce Wayne shows Dick Grayson his impressive vintage motorcycle collection, with Dick in his street garb of leather jacket and jeans.

sugar | and spice

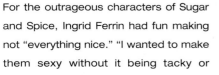

For the outrageous characters of Sugar and Spice, Ingrid Ferrin had fun making not "everything nice." "I wanted to make them sexy without it being tacky or trashy or exposing body parts," she explains. "I just wanted the lines of the costumes to leave everything up to the imagination. Joel wanted Drew Barrymore's Sugar to be just the color of cream, all the soft and delicate things in life; Debi Mazar's Spice is very graphic, sharp-edged

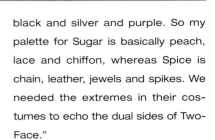

black and silver and purple. So my palette for Sugar is basically peach, lace and chiffon, whereas Spice is chain, leather, jewels and spikes. We needed the extremes in their costumes to echo the dual sides of Two-Face."

Above left: Drew Barrymore , all soft edges as Sugar in the Riddler's Lair. *Above:* Debi Mazar in Spice's more outrageous attire. *Inset:* Spice looming appropriately behind Two-Face's "bad" side.

thugs and
other ruffians

Bob Ringwood made Two-Face's thugs entertainingly demented echoes of their nefarious boss, outfitting them in two-tone ski masks, big black leather boots, and piercing various parts of their anatomy. These are not the kind of fellows you want to bring home to mother.

And neither are the members of the Gotham street gang who take on Dick (and ultimately Batman) in a day-glo alleyway. Says Ringwood, "Joel wanted them to be sort of the essence of all gang members, a generic international gang with a bit of everything. Hoodlums of all nations, as it were. I figured that with the ultra-violet used in the scene, the day-glo fringing and feathers hanging off them would move a lot in the light. That was an idea that happened at the last minute, but sometimes if you've got no time at all to do something, you come up with something that's quite fun. If you have too long to think about it, you get stale."

Below: A magical confluence of imaginative costuming, makeup and hair design, amply demonstrated by the day-glo street gang in the downtown Gotham alley. *Far right:* Martial arts star, Don "The Dragon" Wilson, brilliantly unrecognizable as the gang leader. *Right:* Two-Face's thugs in action at the Nygmatech party.

very special
effects

an interview with john dykstra

There are few figures in the world of special visual effects as distinguished, innovative and even visionary as John Dykstra. And there have been few films to utilize his talents so expansively as *Batman Forever*, which required visual effects so unique that state-of-the-art-of-*tomorrow* would be an apt description.

Dykstra was born in Long Beach, California, where, coincidentally, much of *Batman Forever* would be shot in the Dome (the old Hughes aircraft hanger that formerly housed the Spruce Goose). He was a stills photographer while attending design school, and got his start in film by collaborating on the special effects for Douglas Trumbull's low-budget but impressive 1972 ecological science fiction film *Silent Running*. The following year he went to work for Berkeley's Institute of Urban Development, where he participated in a sophisticated project applying cinematography and visual effects to the construction of miniature cityscape models (a task which would certainly come into play for the building of Gotham City).

Dykstra re-entered films triumphantly as the innovative special effects supervisor on George Lucas' classic *Star Wars* in 1977, winning two Academy Awards, one for the invention and development of the Dykstraflex motion-control camera system. For *Star Wars*, Dykstra served as the first head of Lucas' renowned visual effects company, Industrial Light and Magic (ILM).

Right: Oscar-winning visual effects supervisor John Dykstra. *Below:* The massive Dome in Long Beach that served as a primary studio for *Batman Forever*. *Bottom:* The Batmobile rising in the Batcave, a set built inside the Dome.

Above: The Batcave in flames, thanks to the Rloder (inset) and special effects supervisor Tommy Fisher. *Left:* Rick Baker adjusts one of his ingenious articulated bats.

Dykstra left ILM to form his own company, Apogee, through which he produced the first five television episodes and the motion picture version of *Battlestar Galactica* in 1979. He received another Academy Award nomination for Robert Wise's *Star Trek - The Motion Picture*, also in 1979. Since then, Dykstra has overseen visual effects for several more films, and has continued to research ever more innovative methods of bringing the impossible to "reality."

Dykstra was not alone in the quest to make *Batman Forever* one of the most imaginative effects films of its time. Handling special physical effects – everything from an exploding Batcave to a collapsing abandoned subway station to the revolving carport for the Batmobile – was Thomas L. (Tommy) Fisher. A man who knows his way around every aspect of special effects, Fisher recently performed groundbreaking work on James Cameron's *Terminator 2: Judgment Day* and *True Lies*, the latter earning him a 1994 Academy Award nomination. His other credits include a number of big-budget action films famed for their ingenious pyrotechnics, including *Rambo: First Blood Part II*, *Rambo III*, *Total Recall*, *The Last of the Mohicans* and *Under Siege*.

Rick Baker is another special effects wizard who made his own contributions, including extensive special effects makeup and two remarkably realistic, mechanically articulated bats. Baker won Oscars for both *An American Werewolf in London* and *Harry and the Hendersons* and received nominations for *Greystoke: The Legend of Tarzan, Lord of the Apes*, *Coming to America* and, in 1994, *Ed Wood*. Baker's other feature credits have included *King Kong*, *Star Wars*, *Gorillas in the Mist*, *Gremlins 2: The New Batch* and *Wolf*. For television, Baker won a Best Makeup Emmy Award for *The Autobiography of Miss Jane Pittman*.

Toward the end of principal photography on *Batman Forever*, maestro Dykstra found time to explain to the author some of the visual effects wonders that he was creating for the film:

MICHAEL SINGER: It seems to me that your work for *Batman Forever* calls upon the entire range of technology that exists in visual effects today.

JOHN DYKSTRA: We've been charged by the script and the creative team to make something that is visually envelope-breaking. We want to present images that actually do challenge today's technologies. We're going to be using motion control, which is the ability to duplicate the movement of the camera in several different situations and then combine those separate pieces of film into a single scene to make them look as though they had occurred at one time. We will be using a motion capture technique, which means that we can operate the camera freely when we're shooting live action, and then having recorded that motion, again duplicate that motion in a miniature environment. We will also be using that data to combine original photography of miniatures and live action with computer-generated components. We will be creating a comic book feel to this. Batman will be larger than life, and the environment in which he exists will have larger-than-life perspectives, dimensions and lighting. It will also have a surrealistic and visceral feel. In *Batman Forever*, we're forcing the limits of reality. We're going to create our own reality!

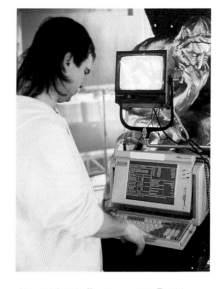

Above: Visual effects operator David Stump with his motion capture computer – especially designed for the film – in the Riddler's Lair. *Below:* Robin hauls Batman from the ruins of the Gotham Plaza subway station, after it was collapsed by Tommy Fisher's physical effects crew.

MS: You have to have an extraordinary amount of co-ordination with Barbara Ling's art department, because when you're creating cityscapes inside the computer, it has to be consistent with Barbara's and Joel's vision of Gotham. How difficult is that?

JD: It's a prerequisite that you have collaboration. And as a result, every facet of the work that we are doing is storyboarded to anticipate the components that we're going to have to photograph and the

participation of the individuals who will provide those components. Although we will be using miniatures for part of our city and will be using CGI (computer-generated imagery) for another part, we truly are getting to design Gotham pretty much from scratch. The city has become more vertical and has incorporated into it many more levels of traffic. Bridges cross at high levels. It's beyond the ability of contemporary architecture to build, but there are elements of styles past, present and future.

MS: How many visual effects shots will *Batman Forever* require?

JD: My guess is that it will be someplace in the neighborhood of 200 or more.

MS: That's a lot for any movie. How many effects shots did *Star Wars* have?

JD: I think *Star Wars* had 240, and *Jurassic Park* had about 200. In contemporary terms, visual effects movies tend to have many more shots than they used to because the audience has become much more sophisticated. And the traditional illusions that motion pictures have used to sort of sleight-of-hand the audience have been done so frequently that your feet are put to the fire to come up with something new. So we're being asked to make many of the shots that might have been done conventionally in the past in a new and different way in order to go beyond the threshold which has been established for the audience ... and make them even more exciting.

gotham cybercity

MS: Is it possible to give any examples of how you're going to "push the envelope"?

JD: Well, I think the computer-generated city is certainly one of them. Although facets of cities have been generated in films past, this is going to be, I think, one of the most extensive definitions of a city that a computer's ever been asked to do. And along with that, and in the same breath, I must say that we're also creating extensive miniatures to support the computer-generated images.

In one challenging sequence, we're going to fly through the city. And it will incorporate elements of miniatures, live action and CGI, all in one shot! And the blending of those elements, and the matching of the lens

distortions and color and contrast are going to be critical. In the shot, we rise up through the city. The Batmobile drives by. We continue to rise and pass a bridge, and on that bridge the Batmobile drives by again, and we ascend even further and pass another bridge, then tilt up to discover the skyline of Gotham. It's twice as tall as New York and has an incredible amount of architectural detail and design. And we find the Bat-Signal in the sky! That one shot is going to incorporate virtually every technique and technology that is being used in visual effects today.

MS: What other elaborate shots can you discuss at this point?

JD: The camera will approach Gotham aerially to view an all computer-generated city, with computer-generated water, smoke, reflections. That's a shot where we're really dealing with computer-

Above: This magnificent image from Warner Bros. Imaging Technology of Gotham Police cars driving past the exterior of Two-Face's secret hideout is an ingenious composite of live action (the police cars were filmed driving past the base of Manhattan Bridge in New York) and digital matte painting (the sculpted head and upper portion of the bridge, the graffiti, lighting and coloration effects). *Left:* Photograph of Wall Street in New York City converted by computer graphics artist Mary Locatell into a conceptual image of Gotham City (*far left*), which then inspired the "real" Gotham created by Barbara Ling and John Dykstra.

A beautiful example of digital artistry from Warner Bros. Imaging Technology, as the Ritz Gotham Hotel exterior is wholly created in the computer. Utilizing the real U.S. Customs building in New York as the foundation, artists then extended the facade into an imaginary but incredibly realistic skyscraper. Here we see the early wire frame (*top*), the interim quick render (*center*) and then the final render of the imposing structure (*bottom*). *Above right*: Another extraordinary image from WBIT that combines digitized imagery (the Gotham cityscape and Wayne Enterprises facade) with a live action element (the interior of Bruce Wayne's office beyond the circular window).

generated objects, three dimensional models in a virtual space. But the most challenging shots are the ones where we try to integrate different elements into one shot.

MS: It's incredible to think about the number of people you're working with to make all of this happen.

JD: So many people are integral to this movie, and it couldn't be done without them. Eric Durst is working on the Second Bank of Gotham heist scene; Boyd Shermis is doing the Batwing sequence in the approach to Claw Island; David Stump is on stage every day with a live-action crew making certain that when something comes up, he's there to solve the problems for them in CGI; James Hegedus is our representative in the art department; Jo Ann Knox is doing the production supervision. Each one of these people – and more I haven't mentioned – are being asked to do more than what they've ever done before, either faster or better or both. All the technologies, the computers, are only tools. It's like a hammer in the hands of a carpenter.

the miniatures

MS: Talk a little about the miniatures you've been shooting in the old Hughes Aircraft hangars in Playa del Rey.

JD: Gotham in miniature is about 100 feet long, 25-50 feet wide and up to 50 feet tall. And we're only looking at the upper half of Gotham in these miniatures. We've also got a Batmobile in ⅛th scale, about 4 feet long; two scales of Batwings, one nearly 12 feet long and almost as wide and another at ½th scale and a miniature Batboat as well.

MS: Do you see this project as being the most challenging you've had since *Star Wars*?

JD: Oh yeah, by far.

MS: How on earth do you create all this in the amount of time that you're allotted to do it in?

JD: I have had to completely re-evaluate and re-organize

my thinking about how I do things. When I was first involved in this
business, if you came to understand lenses, cameras and film and how
light worked in them, you had all of the tools you needed to produce
startling photographic imagery. And everyone worked under the same
constraints. With the advent of the creation of images in virtual environments, we have opened a completely new venue for the production of
images. And it is change. It is not computers, it is not just cameras. It is
change. You have to be constantly ready to adapt to some new
technique. Let's say we were going to spend a year working on a film.
If at the beginning you set out to use known technologies to do your film,
you will be obsolete by the time your film comes out a year later. So what
you must do is constantly risk. You must assume that a technology which
has not been developed is going to happen. And you've got to assume
that it's going to happen before you finish your picture.

So, change is the key. Constant adaptation. You have to stay light
on your feet. You can't do it the easy way. You have to find ways of not
making effects more complex or difficult or expensive, but to make them
more *exciting*.

Below: A high-angle view of a Gotham City miniature cityscape ready to be filmed.
Right: Another view of Gotham in miniature which demonstrates its incredible realism. *Inset
top and bottom:* Artists and technicians at work on two of the miniature skyscrapers.

vehicles, gadgets and arsenals

For the new vision of Batman conjured up by Joel Schumacher and the other creative talents of *Batman Forever*, newly conceived vehicles, gadgets and arsenals had to follow. Nothing, but nothing, would be the same as in the previous films, and that includes the most famous asset of all...

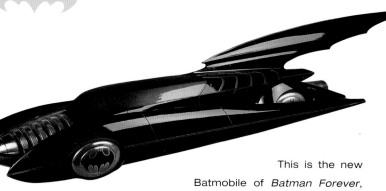

the batmobile

Beyond sleek. Organic. Sinuous. Powerful interior machinery radiating with blue-white light through a ribbed body, wing and fins rising majestically from the rear of its body, illuminated hubcaps emblazoned with the Bat Ensignia, a powerful engine pulsating beneath the meshed hood, an orange-red flame jetting out of the rear turbine exhaust, its matte finish as black as the Gotham night. Gorgeous and terrifying, its like has never been seen before.

Left: The Batmobile roars down a Gotham street, spewing its impressive turbine exhaust. *Top right and right:* Two of the four early Batmobile models designed by Barbara Ling and her team before the final version evolved. *Bottom:* The final Batmobile on its Batcave platform. *Inset:* Original drawing by Tim Flattery of the Batmobile in its near-completed state.

This is the new Batmobile of *Batman Forever*, and it's the result of months of trial and error, experimentation and testing, before perfection was achieved. Production designer Barbara Ling worked closely on the Batmobile with art department illustrator Tim Flattery, an expert in vehicle design, and special effects supervisor Tommy Fisher, who would build the chassis, as well as Allen Pike and Charley Zurian of TFX, a company that specializes in the construction of unique vehicles.

"The Batmobile was quite a challenge," says Barbara Ling, "and we actually went through many stages

to get to our final vehicle. The first thing I knew that I wanted was to have that wing on top, which would help the car resemble the silhouette of a bat. After going through several concepts with Joel Schumacher, we came up with four different looks as finalists: three very much machine-age and one which we called the Stealth, because it looked like a Stealth bomber adapted as a car with the winged fin on top."

"We built these four as clay models," continues Tim Flattery, "and at first, Joel chose the Stealth model. But a short time later, he realized that if you took the wing off the top, it would look too much like a normal car, and the Batmobile had to be something spectacular. It's the Batmobile, after all ... it had to be its own entity. And Joel was absolutely right about that."

Ling found the inspiration for the final version of the Batmobile in a videotape of a bat flying in a wind tunnel. "The bat is an amazing animal," says Ling. "The structure of its wings, its veins and ribs. So we went back to the drawing board, and started going for a stylized, automotive version of a bat. I wanted the Batmobile to look like a living, breathing thing, and you cannot believe how hard it is to design it, and then make it work. I give TFX, Tommy Fisher and Tim Flattery great kudos for working out the technical aspects."

The Batmobile took four

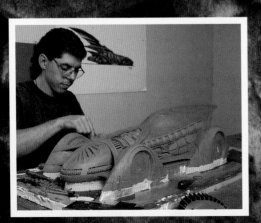

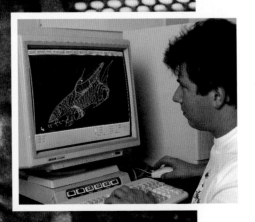

Main picture: The Batmobile primed in the Batcave for its next mission. *Center, bottom left and right:* Stages of construction for the Batmobile at the TFX workshop, full-sized, minature and computer design.

months to build from the first sketch to the finished product, not a lot of time for such an ambitious high-tech project. Whereas the previous Batmobiles were constructed from fiberglass, Ling, Flattery, Pike and Zurian sought to make the new one from some of the most durable materials available. Carbon fiber – the same material used for Formula One racing cars and F-16 jet fighters – went into the body of the Batmobile, along with a high-temperature epoxy resin with all of the air extracted through vacuum bagging. "It makes it really super lightweight and super-strong," notes Allen Pike. "In fact, if Batman were a real person, and the Batmobile a real car, this is probably what it would be built from." Tim Flattery adds: "It could stop bullets!"

The Batmobile is outfitted with a powerful ZZ3 Chevrolet racing engine, capable of far exceeding 100 mph in reality. In the film, its speed will appear to be considerably greater. The car's dimensions, including the wing, is 25 feet-long, and 10½ feet-high. That's a lot of Batmobile!

the batwing
batboat and batsub

Batman's other vehicles share a consistent organic design with the Batmobile, making them all truly of a collective piece. The **Batwing** in *Batman Forever* has been completely redesigned by Barbara Ling with illustrator Matt Codd from the version seen in the first Batman film. It is now swifter, sharper, and more dynamic. Constructed in miniature by John Dykstra's visual effects crew, the new Batwing was then put through its swooping, gliding paces through the magic of Dykstra's virtual reality, his famed motion control techniques and also through computerized composites.

The **Batboat** was another vehicle designed by Barbara Ling with Tim Flattery's assistance. "We took the Batmobile and incorporated elements of it into the Batboat, and then got a marine expert to make sure that we designed a hull that was seaworthy," explains Flattery. The jet-driven Batboat was an extraordinary sight on the open sea: 30-foot-high "rooster tails," plumes of water

An all new Batwing was developed for Batman Forever. Above right: A superb production design painting by Matt Codd. Right: The Batwing in miniature.

Above: Robin joins Batman and Alfred in the Subterranean Batcave as he prepares to roar off in the waiting Batboat.
Inset: A schematic from TFX who constructed the Batboat.
Right: A 1950s Studebaker serves as a Gotham police car.

spraying into the night sky, with the turbine exhaust between them blasting flame. Like the Batmobile, the mechanical innards radiate light through the ribs, lending the Batboat the appearance of a great sea monster cascading through the brine.

The **Batsub** is one of the Dark Knight's secret weapons. No machine is indestructible, but when the Batwing is blown out of the skies, it re-emerges as the Batsub with even greater force under the sea. Remarkably, the Batsub was created entirely as a computer-generated image.

There are other vehicles featured in *Batman Forever*. Two-Face and his thugs do their dirty deeds in a menacing vintage 1940s armored car. Two-Face's Helicopter is decorated with the villain's trademark yin/yang symbol. Barbara Ling actually found a real Bell chopper body in pieces, which was then re-assembled like a giant plastic model and mounted on a gigantic hydraulic platform for filming.

Edward Nygma tools around in his characteristically strange bicycle (designed by property master Brad Einhorn). Gothamites travel in a bizarre array of cars dating from the 1950s, '60s and '70s; Gotham Police cars are black and blue 1950s Studebakers with colorfully blinking lights on their roofs; the Gotham City Cab Service (call Gotham 6-4408 for service) utilizes old New York Checkers cabs painted black, with a miniature, illuminat-

ed Gotham cityscape on their roofs indicating whether they're in service or not.

Bruce Wayne prefers either to drive a hip '60s Jaguar sportster, or to be chauffeured by Alfred in a 1962 Bentley. Dick Grayson, who's a devotee of great motorcycles, roars around town on a 1974 Norton. He also admires Bruce's collection of vintage bikes, which include a 1950 Ariel, 1917 military-style Harley Davidson, a 1954 Vincent Black Knight (of which only 100 were made), a 1947 Indian and a 1920s Pope. All of these glorious vehicles were secured by transportation coordinator Craig Pinkard, thanks to collectors around the country.

Bruce – who also knows the value of great ride – also flies to the Wayne Enterprises headquarters in a richly appointed Augusta 109 helicopter, one of which was transferred to Universal Studios Stage 12 for filming. But when he needs a fast trip from his office directly into the Batcave to swing into action, Wayne utilizes his supersonic luge, zooming through metallic tunnels beneath the streets of Gotham.

gadgets from
batman's vault

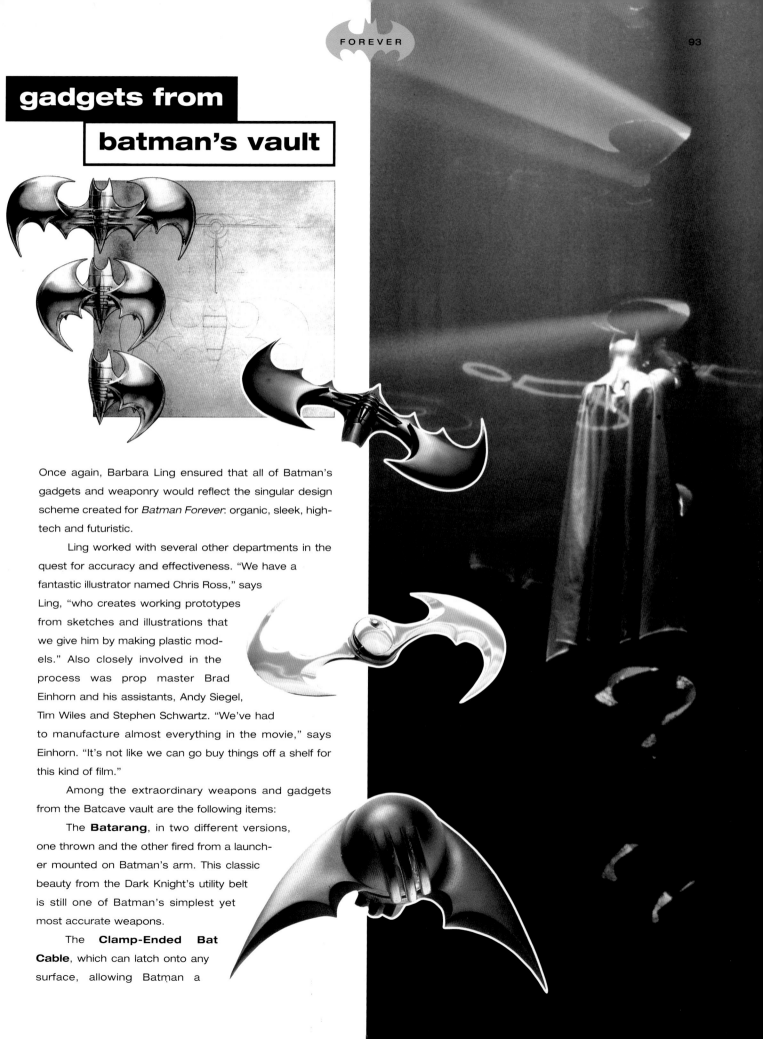

Once again, Barbara Ling ensured that all of Batman's gadgets and weaponry would reflect the singular design scheme created for *Batman Forever*: organic, sleek, high-tech and futuristic.

Ling worked with several other departments in the quest for accuracy and effectiveness. "We have a fantastic illustrator named Chris Ross," says Ling, "who creates working prototypes from sketches and illustrations that we give him by making plastic mod-els." Also closely involved in the process was prop master Brad Einhorn and his assistants, Andy Siegel, Tim Wiles and Stephen Schwartz. "We've had to manufacture almost everything in the movie," says Einhorn. "It's not like we can go buy things off a shelf for this kind of film."

Among the extraordinary weapons and gadgets from the Batcave vault are the following items:

The **Batarang**, in two different versions, one thrown and the other fired from a launch-er mounted on Batman's arm. This classic beauty from the Dark Knight's utility belt is still one of Batman's simplest yet most accurate weapons.

The **Clamp-Ended Bat Cable**, which can latch onto any surface, allowing Batman a

chance to climb into places which would otherwise be unreachable.

The **Bat Bolo**, which can be used by Batman to trip up crimebreakers with its tiny, whirring cables.

The **Bat Torch**, its tiny blue-hot flame capable of burning through even the toughest materials.

The **Bat Grapple Hook**, which can be fired into stone or steel to give Batman the ability to then climb or swing into action on a strong cable which is attached to the hook.

The **Bat Goo Gun**, a nifty device which shoots out an iridescent substance that stops crimebreakers in their tracks.

two-face and
the riddler's
armaments
and gadgets

From standard **pistols** to a **flame gun** and **rocket launcher**, Two-Face maintains an interesting and nasty assortment of oversized guns, all of them especially built by Einhorn and his crew for the film.

Two-Face's gang of masked thugs wield ferocious, old-fashioned **tommy guns** futurized with circular, neon-lit magazines. They're the kind of guns that only muscle-bound, muscle-headed scoundrels could love.

Of course, Two-Face also has his most benign-looking but dangerous weapon: his famous **coin**, with one clean and one scratched side. The flip of this coin determines the fate of Two-Face's adversaries, and heaven help the poor soul who winds up on the "bad" side of that coin!

Chris Ross illustrated all of Batman's and Two-Face's gadgets and weapons, and Jim Carson worked

on the concepts for the Riddler's materiel. The Riddler's primary gadget, of course, is his famous **cane**, which Jim Carrey wielded with the facility of an award-winning baton-twirler. There are two versions of the cane in the film: the first manifestation, wherein the question-mark-shaped handle clicks open to reveal an electronic console with buttons that can perform a variety of functions (like opening a locked door to the Batcave). The second, even more sinister cane, was designed for the Riddler in his "advanced" state of being, when his brain power and delusions of grandeur are at their height. This version has a skull tip with a sole green button, with which the Riddler can create further havoc.

To lay waste to the Batcave, the Riddler dips into a sack and pulls out his little, wind-up toy **Batty Bombs**. These

Top left: The Bat Grapple Hook and hand-held launcher. *Top right:* One of the beautfiully constructed riddles sent out by the Riddler. *Above:* Two-Face's handgun. *Below:* The Riddler and his trademark gold cane with its control panel on view.

tiny balls of destruction flap their diminutive wings, their question mark-festooned bodies clearly indicating from whence they came. They may not look like weapons, but the Riddler's **riddles** are missives of mischief, each marvelously constructed and mechanically articulated. For these, Jim Carson did the prototypes and Brad Einhorn had them built. "Some of them are like elaborate pop-up cards," says Einhorn, "and some of them work with little motors. They were a lot of fun to do."

Finally – although not a conventional weapon by any means – there is the Riddler's ultimate gadget, the Remote Encephalographic Stimulator Box, or more simply, just **the Box**. This brilliant but warped invention – which beams TV signals directly into the human brain, and then beams the contents of the viewers' brains back to the Riddler – sets much of the plot of *Batman Forever* in motion. The invention progresses from its clunky prototype to the sleeker version that's marketed for mass consumption (not to mention the Riddler's portable "brain sucker"), all thanks to production designer Ling, propmaster Einhorn and effectsman Fisher, who creatively collaborat-

ed on the different stages of the mad invention. After the live scenes were shot, John Dykstra would then add remarkable digital effects that completed the illusion of the Box in action.

The Box is humorously designed, intentionally resembling an electric blender gone berserk, its green glow and revolving fins looking more comical than terrifying. The version which is packaged and sold in the movie's electronics stores resembles a television set with an extra added attraction. ("Not just a television, but a whole experience!" trumpets the box that it's sold in: "20 Inch Virtual Reality Screen ... 300 Watt Envelop-Sound Processor ... Built-In Nygmatech Reality Synthesizer ... Cyberwave Remote Control ... Genuine Ebony Veneer.")

Like "normal" television itself, the Box only looks harmless! But little do the good people of Gotham know the evil that lurks within....

Above and center: Two more of the stunning riddles made by Jim Carson and Brad Einhorn for the movie. *Top right:* The Riddler's wind up Batty Bombs which he used to destroy the Batcave. *Above:* Alfred and Bruce Wayne study Edward Nygma's "Box", devised to suck out the brain power of anyone who uses it. *Right:* Edward Nygma uses his prototype Remote Encephalographic Stimulator on his luckless boss, Fred Stickley.

CAST LIST

Bruce Wayne/Dick Grayson	**Val Kilmer**
Harvey Dent/Two-Face	**Tommy Lee Jones**
Edward Nygma/The Riddler	**Jim Carrey**
Dr. Chase Meridian	**Nicole Kidman**
Dick Grayson/Robin	**Chris O'Donnell**
Alfred	**Michael Gough**
Commissioner Gordon	**Pat Hingle**
Sugar	**Drew Barrymore**
Spice	**Debi Mazar**
Fred Stickley	**Ed Begley, Jr.**

CREW LIST

Director	Joel Schumacher
Producers	Tim Burton
	Peter Macgregor-Scott
Executive Producers	Benjamin Melniker
	Michael Uslan
Screenwriters	Lee Batchler
	& Janet Scott Batchler
	and Akiva Goldsman
Director of Photography	Stephen Goldblatt
Production Designer	Barbara Ling
Art Directors	Chris Burian-Mohr,
	James Hegedus,
	Joseph P. Lucky
Set Decorator	Elise "Cricket" Rowland
Costume Designers	Bob Ringwood and
	Ingrid Ferrin
Music	Elliot Goldenthal
Film Editor	Dennis Virkler
First Assistant Director	Bill Elvin
Sound Mixer	Petur Hliddal
Key Makeup Artist	Ve Neill
Key Hair Stylist	Yolanda Toussieng
Visual Effects Supervisor	John Dykstra
Stunt Coordinator	Conrad Palmisano
Special Effects Supervisor	Thomas L. Fisher

CREDITS NOT FINAL

ABOUT THE AUTHOR

Michael Singer is a motion picture unit publicist, author and journalist who previously authored *Batman Returns: The Official Movie Book* and *The Making of Oliver Stone's 'Heaven and Earth'*. For the past 11 years, Singer has edited and authored the annually published industry reference book *Michael Singer's Film Directors: A Complete Guide* – which has also included interviews by Singer with more than 50 prominent filmmakers – and has contributed articles to such publications as *Film Comment, American Cinematographer* and *Films in Review*. In addition to *Batman Forever* and *Batman Returns*, Singer has served as unit publicist on such films as *Natural Born Killers, Heaven and Earth, Grumpy Old Men* and *Free Willy*.

A native of New York City, Singer lives in Los Angeles with his Japanese-born wife, Yuko, and their baby daughter, Miyako.

ABOUT THE PHOTOGRAPHER

Ralph Nelson was the unit photographer for *Batman Forever*. His photographs have been seen in books about the making of the three *Back to the Future* films, *Return of the Jedi* and *Bram Stoker's Dracula*. Nelson has also served as unit photographer on such notable films as *Nine to Five, Gremlins, Indiana Jones and the Temple of Doom* (U.S. portion), *WarGames, Tucker: The Man and his Dream, Top Gun, Basic Instinct*, and *The Shadow*.

Other artwork/photos by Michael Garland, Jane O'Neal, Virgil Mirano, the *Batman Forever* Art Department, the *Batman Forever* Visual Effects Department, Warner Bros. Imaging Technology, TFX and DC Comics.